S. Prakash Sethi and Dow Votaw, *editors*

THE PRENTICE-HALL SERIES
IN ECONOMIC INSTITUTIONS AND SO(

Private Management and Public Policy

THE PRINCIPLE OF PUBLIC RESPONSIBILITY

Lee E. Preston
State University of New York at Buffalo

James E. Post
Boston University

PRENTICE-HALL, INC., *Englewood Cliffs, New Jersey*

Library of Congress Cataloging in Publication Data

Preston, Lee E
    Private management and public policy.

    (Prentice-Hall series in economic institutions and social systems)
    Includes bibliographical references and index.
    1. Industry—Social aspects. 2. Industry—Social aspects—United
States. I. Post, James E., joint author. II. Title.
HD60.P73   658.4'08   74-26551
ISBN 0-13-710988-1
ISBN 0-13-710970-9 pbk.

Printed in the United States of America

10 9 8 7 6 5 4 3 2 1

PRENTICE-HALL INTERNATIONAL, Inc., *London*
PRENTICE-HALL OF AUSTRALIA, Pty. Ltd., *Sydney*
PRENTICE-HALL OF CANADA, Ltd., *Toronto*
PRENTICE-HALL OF INDIA PRIVATE LIMITED, *New Delhi*
PRENTICE-HALL OF JAPAN, Inc., *Tokyo*

To the memory
of
ELI GOLDSTON

Contents

Foreword

After having been a part of the curriculum in many schools of business for twenty years or more, the field now vaguely described as "business and society" seems at last to be coming into focus. A common core of interest has begun to evolve and to give promise of providing the integrating concepts of teaching and research that have been so conspicuous by their absence in the past. Evidence of this long delayed crystallization can be found in new course descriptions and outlines, in the research interests of those working in the field, and in the proceedings of conferences convened for the purpose of examining the proper content and parameters of this important area of practical, as well as academic, concern. The field and its integrating theme appear very clearly, as suggested above, to be the complex, dynamic, two-way relationship between the economic institutions of our society, with which most schools of business are primarily concerned, and the social systems in which those institutions now operate and are likely to operate in the future.

It would be incorrect and misleading to suggest that the interaction between business and society has not been a part of the business school curriculum in the past. In one form or another, this interaction has played an important role in business and society courses for many years. There are, however, several basic differences between what has been done in the past and the new rallying point we now see evolving. The old, and still dominant, approach has been very narrow in its emphasis and in its boundaries and has all too often been limited to little more than an instructor's particular specialty in such areas as social control, business and government, or antitrust. Even where an instructor's narrow predispositions are not present, the "social" side of the relationship is often viewed as being static, or relatively so, and external to the current decision or situational context; and the primary goals of the course are those of explaining the phenomenon of business to the students and of analyzing the requirements of business-like, efficient, or responsible behavior in a rather loose social sense. Furthermore, the emphasis is almost wholly the private, large, and industrial aspects of the economic sector, with little, if any, attention devoted to the public, small, or nonindustrial variables.

The flaws in this approach are obvious, and changes are already beginning to take place. What appears to be evolving, and what we believe should be evolving, is a much greater interest in the dynamics of the whole system. What is needed is a systematic analysis of the effects (noneconomic as well as economic) of business on other institutions and on the social system, and of the effects of changes in other institutions and in the social system on the economic sector. Most important, perhaps, the stage should be set for an understanding of the basic assumptions, attitudes, values, concepts, and ideologies that underlie a particular arrangement of economic institutions and social systems and of how changes in these assumptions affect the arrangements and the interactions among the various parts of the whole system.

Two other points ought also to be made here. *First,* although most schools of business do not behave as though it were so, they are actually engaged in training the managers of tomorrow and not the managers of today. As the relationships between economic institutions and their social environment become more intimate and as each part of the whole system becomes more sensitive and more responsive to changes in the other parts, how much more important it is going to be for the manager to understand the dynamics of the system as a whole than it is for him to know what the momentary conformation happened to be when he was in school. It seems to us, further, that one of the manifestations of an industrially mature society will be the economic sector's diminishing importance and, as a consequence, a reversal of the flow of influence from the economic sector to society as a whole. The manager of the future will need to be more sensitive to changes in society than he ever was in the past. His training will have to include a very different congeries of tools and ingredients than it now does.

Second, we think note should be taken of some evidence now beginning to accumulate that suggests that in the future schools of business may come to play the same sort of influential role in the profession of management that schools of law and medicine now play in theirs. If this change should come about, it will become even more important that managers, during their period of formal education, be provided with those conceptual and analytical tools that best meet the needs of their profession and of the society as a whole. If present forecasts prove to be accurate and "continuing education" becomes a much more important aspect of higher education than it is now, among the first academic institutions to be profoundly affected will be the schools of business. The influence of the schools upon the profession of management will become more immediate and the need for pragmatic training in the interactions between economic institutions and social systems greatly enhanced.

While there is no great disagreement on these general issues, it would be a mistake to assume that there is consensus on the details. We believe that this series takes into account both the agreement on some of the broader points and the lack of consensus on many of the more specific aspects of the changes taking place in the environmental field. For example, there are people who believe that comments like those made above dictate the integration of social materials in all parts of the business curriculum rather than their use in specialized courses devoted to the field; there are many who feel that the bulk of such work should be done in specialized courses; there are many views in the area between these two extremes. We feel that this series is designed in such a way that it can cater to business school curricula of all varieties.

We visualize this series evolving in a set of concentric circles starting at the core and expanding outward. The innermost circle consists of those books that provide much of the basic material that is usually included in the introductory courses in "business and society," including the institutional role of large corporations; government interaction with business; business ideology and values; methodological approaches to measuring the social impact of business activities; corporations and political activities; and the influence of corporate management on the formulation of public policy.

The next circle is made up of books that deal with the impact of corporate activities in specific functional areas. The issues covered here include marketing and social conflict; accounting, accountability, and the public interest; corporate personnel policies and individual rights; and computers and invasion of privacy.

The outermost circle consists of books that are either interdisciplinary or cross-cultural in nature or both. Here we are concerned with the synergistic effect of various economic activities on the society as a whole. On one dimension we are concerned with issues such as how technology gets introduced into society; the economic effects of various types of social welfare programs; how various social activities like health, sanitation, mass transit, and public education are affected by the actions of business; and the social consequences of zero economic growth or population growth. On another level, studies will include comparison between corporate behavior in different social systems.

The concentric circles are not intended to be mutually exclusive, nor do they reflect a certain order of priority in the nature of problems or publication schedule. They are simply a convenient arrangement for thinking about the relationships among various problem areas.

In addition to their role as part of the training provided by collegiate schools of business and management and other social science disciplines, most of the volumes in the series are also of use and interest to managers and to the general public. The basic purpose of the series is to help provide a better understanding of the relationship between our economic institutions and the broader social system, and it is obvious that the need which the series hopes to satisfy is not confined to students of business and management or for that matter even to students. The ultimate goal, we suppose, is not just better corporate social policy but better public policy as well, in the formation of which all citizens participate. Consequently, we have urged the authors of these volumes to keep in mind the broad, in addition to the narrow, targets and to couch their work in language, content, and style that meet both kinds of requirements.

S. Prakash Sethi
Dow Votaw

University of California
Berkeley, California

Acknowledgments

It seems that this book was writing itself in the back of our minds a long time before we became aware of it. The form of the argument began to take shape in our teaching and conversation, and was particularly stimulated by the development of a new course, "The Public Policy Environment of Management," as part of the MBA program at Buffalo. Professors Joseph Shister and C. Perry Bliss contributed importantly to that project, and Professor Phillip Ross joined in teaching the course from time to time. Ideas and viewpoints from each of these colleagues—and reactions from students in this and other courses—have been freely woven into this manuscript with no attempt at attribution.

Professors Dow Votaw and S. Prakash Sethi also share responsibility for this volume in both direct and indirect ways. Long personal association with them, and continuing exposure to their evolving ideas and publications, underlies much of our own analysis. The book itself was written in response to their invitation, and it has benefited greatly from their specific criticisms and suggestions. The manuscript also received careful and valuable scrutiny from Professor Robert Chatov, and numerous specific suggestions and queries came from other colleagues and students as the work proceeded.

All of these individuals are welcome to claim credit for any part of the resulting presentation that they like and can recognize as their own. For our failure to meet their criticisms—well, they can write their own books, or even reviews of this one! We thank them warmly for their interest, time, and patience.

The program of activities concerning management-society relationships at the School of Management in Buffalo has been financially supported by a continuing grant from the General Electric Foundation. Some of the work and materials used in preparing this study, as well as the Workshop in which it has been discussed with student and faculty colleagues, were made possible as a result of this support, for which we are duly grateful.

The manuscript was typed (despite redrafts, misplaced references, and scribbled insertions) by Miss Elaine Dicky. She deserves a rest.

L.E.P. / J.E.P.

CHAPTER ONE

Issues and Definitions

An Overview of the Argument

Some Definitions

Management
Managerial Organizations
Society
Social Involvement
Public Policy

Summary

The social responsibility of business is to increase its profits. *Milton Friedman*

• • •

It is the duty of the man of wealth to consider all surplus revenues . . . . as trust funds, which he is called upon to administer . . . . for his poorer brethren, ... doing for them better than they would or could do for themselves.
                                                                Andrew Carnegie

• • •

The duty of business in a democracy is . . . . to follow the social obligations which are defined by the whole community . . . .   *Howard Bowen*

What is, in fact, the purpose and role of private business management in our society? Is it, as Friedman contends, simply to meet the tests of the marketplace and thereby "increase its profits"? Or is it, as Bowen argues, to meet a wide range of social performance goals "defined by the whole community"? Even a casual scanning of current business periodicals and corporate press releases suggests that the latter viewpoint is gradually replacing the former. As a recent *Fortune* article notes, "The doctrine that business has responsibilities 'beyond business' . . . . is still picking up steam." [1]

---

[1]Gilbert Burck, "The Hazards of 'Corporate Responsibility,' " *Fortune*, June, 1973, p. 114.

But changes in official corporate rhetoric, and a wide variety of specific policy initiatives and activities on the part of individual corporations and industries, do not dispose of the basic questions themselves. Indeed, the more seriously one takes the idea that balance sheets and income statements do not provide a fully comprehensive basis for evaluating corporate social performance, the more one returns to the basic issues—the social purpose of business activity, the directions and limits of corporate involvement in society, and the objectives and standards to be achieved.

Evidently it is not possible for individual corporations, even very large ones, to take an active role in every sphere of economic and social life. On the other hand, the alternatives of complete withdrawal, mere charitable activity, or *ad hoc* response to specific demands and crises are equally unsatisfactory. Lectured from every viewpoint and confronted with an avalanche of prescriptions and criticisms, the business community is understandably confused and defensive. Little wonder that the whole problem of business involvement in society and what to do about it has come to be referred to as "the corporate dilemma."[2]

AN OVERVIEW OF THE ARGUMENT

In this book we present an analysis of "corporate dilemma" and suggest a basis for resolving it. Our analysis is focused on two fundamental social processes. One is the process of *management* itself; that is, the process of organizing and directing the individual organizational units that perform productive tasks within, and for the benefit of, the larger society. In our own society most of these organizational units are private businesses, and by far the largest part of private business activity is conducted by corporations of substantial size. Hence, managerial processes and problems characteristic of the larger corporate business organization are our primary concern.

The second element in our analysis is the *public policy process.* Through the public policy process the members of society—individuals, organizations, and interest groups—identify issues of public concern, explore conflicting viewpoints, negotiate and bargain, and—if a resolution is reached—establish objectives and select means of obtaining them. In the ongoing process the structure of government and the political mechanism of society are of central importance. Yet, in both origin and impact, the process itself extends far beyond the boundaries of legislative action and direct governmental activity. In particular, since private business organizations account for much of the character and activity of society as a whole, they are also important stimuli, participants, and respondents within the public policy process itself.

Both the public policy process and the managerial process are well-established areas of academic study and practical activity. Social decision making

[2]Dow Votaw and S. Prakash Sethi, *The Corporate Dilemma* (Englewood Cliffs, N.J.: Prentice Hall, Inc., 1973).

has been a principal topic in philosophy since the days of Plato and forms the primary subject matter of modern political science. Private business management has been recognized as an important area of teaching and research for at least a century. Yet the idea that there may be—perhaps even *must* be—a normal and mutually sustaining relationship between the two processes is relatively new and somewhat controversial, at least in the United States. The traditional American view has been that the public and private sectors of economic life are separate and distinct and that there is a "natural predominance of private enterprise in the economic sphere and . . . subordinate role of public initiative in any situation other than manifest national emergency." [3]

Of course, this traditional separation of public and private roles in economic life is itself both a reflection of and a basis for public policy. The delegation of most of the economic tasks of society to independent private enterprises is a social decision of the first magnitude; and many large and powerful business entities have arisen specifically in response to public policy decisions. (One thinks particularly of the railroads and the aerospace industries.) Then, once established, business enterprises have inevitably come to participate in the public policy process in pursuit of their own private organizational advantages and goals. At the same time, the expanding role of government and governmental protection of other groups within society—such as labor unions, consumers, and taxpayers—has resulted in a counterpenetration of public policy into the activities of private management.

The fact of frequent and varied interpenetration and interdependence between private management and public policy is now generally recognized. However, this fact continues to give rise to expressions of surprise and alarm, both by business executives confronted with new public concerns and requirements and by social critics concerned over the prominent role of business interests in political life. Further, instances of interpenetration and interdependence are commonly regarded as exceptions—each based upon special circumstances—to the general rule of independence between micromanagerial and macro-societal decision processes.

Our own analysis takes, and attempts to justify, a different viewpoint. We believe that interpenetration and interdependence between private managerial activity and social policy making are general and inevitable characteristics of modern, organized societies. Although this fundamental state of interrelatedness may contain potentials for danger—both to the managerial unit and to the public interest—it also contains potentials for constructive adaptation and social change. Interrelatedness between private management and public policy is simply a fact of modern social life.

---

[3]Andrew Shonfield, *Modern Capitalism* (New York: Oxford University Press, 1970), p. 298. Shonfield's general analysis, and particularly his contrast between European and American views of private/public sector relationships, provides an extremely useful perspective. Chapter 15, "The Changing Style of Private Enterprise," deals specifically with the subject matter of our own analysis.

On the basis of this viewpoint we raise two fundamental questions:

(1) What is the appropriate *scope* of private managerial responsibility within society; how far is the individual managerial unit supposed to go in anticipating and attempting to deal with social needs and problems?

(2) Within the defined scope, what are the *criteria* of appraisal and evaluation; how do corporate managers, their critics, and the general public distinguish good from bad performance, success from failure?

According to our analysis, the *scope* of managerial responsibility arises directly from the principal economic activity of the enterprise (raising apples, making steel, providing medical care) and all secondary or subsidiary activities ancillary thereto. Thus, the purview of management extends well beyond internal decision making and direct market contacts to include the impact of its activities, both anticipated and unanticipated, desired and undesired, on the larger society. At the same time, the scope of managerial responsibility is bounded; it does *not* extend to aspects of social life not related, either directly or indirectly, to the organization's central activity.

Within the defined scope of managerial responsibility, the *criteria* of appraisal and evaluation, of success and failure, are established both by market forces and by public policy; therefore, the task of anticipating, understanding, evaluating, and responding to public policy developments within the host environment is itself a critical managerial task. Indeed, an understanding of the broad concerns of society embodied in public policy is as necessary to modern management as an understanding of the keys to market success— the sources of demand for products and services, the technological and cost alternatives relevant to the production activities. Changes in public policy and in the stimuli or limitations placed by society on the activities of the firm are normal phenomena, comparable to changes in tastes and technology within the corporation's industries and markets, not unprecedented occurrences or intrusions upon managerial prerogatives. Further, since private business units constitute large and important organizational elements within our society, it should be expected that they will initiate and participate in, as well as respond to, the process of social decision making.

Our analysis focuses throughout on the *process* of management-society interaction rather than on any specific list of current social expectations, prohibitions, or standards. Although we refer throughout to examples, both current and historic, of managerial involvement in society and of public policy initiatives, these are illustrative rather than exhaustive. Within our model of the management-society relationship, the specific tasks of private management and the specific objectives of public policy are constantly being discovered, examined, defined, and revised. Our suggested basis for resolving the corporate dilemma, which we term *the principle of public responsibility,* provides a framework for adaptation and change in a changing world.

SOME DEFINITIONS

The remainder of this chapter presents some definitions of terms and concepts used in our analysis. These terms and concepts are significant in themselves, and their presentation at this point serves as a further introduction to the rest of the book, where these ideas are treated at much greater depth and with particular attention to the relationships among them. Here we omit such complexities in order to delineate fundamental concepts and critical distinctions.

Management

The term *management* has two important meanings. It refers both to the *people* who are responsible for making and implementing managerial decisions within micro-organizational units (i.e., to the *managers*, considered collectively and not as individuals) and to the managerial *functions* that these people perform. This combination of structural and functional meanings for the term *management* is not undesirable and should not lead to confusion. Indeed, the double meaning emphasizes the point that managerial functions cannot be seriously thought about without reference to the human beings performing them and that the position of managers within an organizational strucure is ultimately defined not by titles or formal organization charts but by the functions that they perform.

In some general discussions the term management is used interchangeably with "business" or, more abstractly, "the firm." Such usage is specifically avoided here. These latter terms appear to encompass at least the stockholders, and very often the employees, dealers, franchisees, and other associates of private business enterprises. *Management*, however, refers only to those individuals, whether owners or employees, involved in managerial activity at a policy-making level. Our principal focus is on *private* management both because private business firms are the most numerous, and in the aggregate most important, managerial units within our society, and because the distinction between micro-organizational and societal considerations can be most sharply drawn in this context. However, we wish to include nonbusiness management within our analysis whenever relevant and convenient.

Managerial Organizations

Management structures exist and managerial functions are performed within *organizations*. An organization is a means of coordinating the activities of a number of people for the achievement of a common purpose or goal. Organizations generally involve both internal specialization—so that some people perform one activity while others perform another—and a hierarchy of authority and responsibility through which the various specialized activities are coordinated and directed toward the common purpose. [4]

The term *organization* is very broad. Religious groups, social clubs, and the units of political government (as distinguished from government agencies) are important organizational types within our society, but they cannot be described primarily as *managerial* in character. The distinguishing feature of the organizations with which we are concerned is that they are *managed.* They are neither loose associations of amateur enthusiasts nor congregations of the like-minded faithful. Rather, they exhibit explicit organizational structures within which functional roles are sharply differentiated and the direction and scope of authority are defined. Of course, most small managerial units lack formal organization charts, and even in large units with well-defined formal structures the actual flows of information and authority may be substantially different from those set forth in official organization plans. The availability and accuracy of any particular representation of formal organizational structure is not, however, at issue here. The point is simply that a specific internal structure, formal or informal, simple or complex, is characteristic of the managerial organizations with which we are concerned.

Both internally and externally, the structure and function of managerial organizations are based upon the concept of *role specialization* and the resulting need for *coordination* of activity among individuals and units performing specialized roles.[5] The fundamental fact is that the number of different tasks that any one individual or organization is capable of performing is limited. Further, as Adam Smith noted long ago, efficiency in performing individual tasks may be increased by means of specialization and the division of labor. Finally, the more specialized and numerous the separate roles, the more complex and important the coordinating activity required to bring about exchange, balance, or consistency among them.

There are two—and only two—ways in which separate and specialized activities can be coordinated and integrated. There are: *administrative direction* (within organizations) and *exchange transactions* (between organizations).[6] If it is thought that separate specialized activities can be more effec-

---

[4]Edgar H. Schein, *Organizational Psychology* (Englewood Cliffs, N.J.: Prentice-Hall, Inc., 1965),Chap. 2; Amitai Etzioni, *Modern Organizations* (Englewood Cliffs, N.J.: Prentice-Hall, Inc., 1964), Chap. 1.

[5]For a penetrating discussion, see Oliver Williamson, "Markets and Hierarchies: Some Elementary Considerations," *The American Economic Review,* LXIII, No. 2 (1973), 316-25 and his forthcoming volume, *Markets and Hierarchies: Analysis and Antitrust Implications* (New York: The Free Press, 1975).

[6]Even this broad distinction becomes blurred if organizational administration is viewed primarily in terms of inducements and contributions, with each member of the group involved in pseudo-exchange relationships with the organization as a whole or its management. Without challenging the validity of this conception, we wish to place primary emphasis here on the *boundary* between the managerial organization and the rest of society, and hence on the role of administrative direction *within,* and exchange relationships *between,* formally separate organizational entities.

tively or efficiently coordinated through internal management than through market transactions, then managerial organizations—communes, cooperatives, business firms, or public agencies—may be formed to conduct them. Activities may be combined within organizations because of their functional similarity or relatedness, because of their mutually offsetting patterns of instability or risk, or simply because administrative coordination eliminates the cost and uncertainty associated with transactions. Explanations of the growth of managerial organizations in terms of the control of scarce resources, the search for power, and so on, generally turn out upon examination to involve some special case of the cost-reduction principle. In the growth of large and complex organizations, costs and economies associated with risk-reduction, planning and control, and elimination of conflict and competition may be of critical importance.

Of course, even large and rationally managed organizations are capable of making errors. Functions and activities may be added and combined in ways that do not, in the end, yield the economies and benefits anticipated. And the benefits obtained by one organization may impose burdens or costs on another. The point here is that managerial organizations are formed by combining numerous, and usually diverse, specialized activities under a single administrative coordinating mechanism. The collective result of these inter nally coordinated activities serves to define the specialized role of the organization as a whole, and hence serves as the basis for its interaction through exchange transactions with other organizations and with society at large.

The selection of a specialized role for the organization, and hence the creation of a basis for exchange relationships between it and the rest of society, is a fundamental managerial function. Only after this role has been selected can management turn to its operating objective—efficient accomplishment of the specific tasks required. When we look at an existing firm, we see it already engaged in a substantial number of tasks, most of which have become highly routinized; and we can scarcely imagine the circumstances under which the question "Shall we perform these tasks or not?" could be seriously examined. Yet the fact is that most organizations routinely face this question with respect to specific and peripheral activities, and the large and strategic decisions of an organization—including the decision of whether or not to establish itself or to remain in operation—are precisely of this character.

The choice of specialized roles and tasks also determines the pattern of guidance and control required for all subsequent managerial activity. Management involves the imposition of administration *within* the organization in order to accomplish transactions *between* it and others. Hence, internal administration should not only be in some sense "better" (at least from the viewpoint of the management itself) than transactional coordination for the activities within the scope of management, it should also be conducted in such a way as to maintain, if not enhance, the ability of the organization as a whole to engage in transactions with others.

Society

Any short definition of the term *society* is doomed to be trivial, meaningless, or both. In attempting a broad definition, Gross refers to ". . . the great complexity of human beings, groups, and formal organizations, of the subsystems within them, and of the intricate clusters, constellations, and macrosystems into which they combine. . . . A tremendous number of variables interacting simultaneously in many ways produces . . . complex aggregates of smaller systems, with varying degrees of cohesion and integration. Thus any effort to understand a national society requires that one deal with the interrelationships among different kinds of subsystems."[7]

For our own purposes the term *society* refers to an aggregate of cohesive social relationships within which the many different and interlinked components and subsystems have their existence. Cohesiveness is a critical attribute, since it accounts for the continuity of social relationships in spite of internal diversity and even conflict.

General characteristics of societies, apart from cohesiveness and complexity, are difficult to specify. Certain key attributes of our own society, however, are generally recognized and important for the present analysis:

It is a rich society. It generates levels of production and permits levels of investment and consumption, unparalleled in world history.

It is formally democratic and certainly pluralistic. Social and political power is diffused among various groups and interests, each subject to the countervailing authority of others, rather than concentrated in a single social class or institution. In spite of great inequalities of both economic and political power, the basic ideology and long-run historical tendencies of our society have been pluralistic and egalitarian.

It is highly organized. Although it is possible for an individual working alone to initiate new social forces (Ralph Nader is the outstanding recent example), the main activities of our society are conducted by and through relatively large organizations—corporations, governmental bodies and agencies, personal interest groups, and others. These organizations do not simply perform functions *for* society; neither are they simply component *parts* of the larger social system. On the contrary, because of their capacity for independent action and initiative, large organizational units can and do alter the structure of society itself, chart the course of its development, and generate and expend its energies.

It may be well to distinguish here between *society* in general and the political concept of the nation-state. The two are very closely related, and the activities of political government are important means of defining and achieving the goals of society at large. However, the particular governmental unit articulating and implementing a social purpose may be local or

[7]Bertram M. Gross, "Social Systems Accounting," in *Social Indicators,* ed. Raymond A. Bauer (Cambridge, Mass.: Massachusetts Institute of Technology, 1966), p. 171.

regional—or, at the other extreme, international—in scope. Further, it is entirely possible for governmental bodies to adopt standards and pursue goals different from those that might be chosen by many important elements within society at large. Hence, the relationship between *management* and *society* is different from the relationship between "business" and "government" in any strict institutional or legal sense, and the appropriateness of governmental decisions and actions can be appraised with the same skepticism and candor as that applied to the behavior of private managerial units.

Social Involvement

The view that business organization and its larger host society are inherently interrelated and that the scope of managerial responsibility extends to some activities not fully mediated by market contracts recognizes the fact of *social involvement*. We prefer the term *involvement* to the more familiar "social responsibility" because the former is ethically neutral. Actual involvement might be great or little, general or specific, benign or malign. By contrast, "social responsibility" appears to convey some specific—and, in most circles favorable—meaning, although the precise thought intended is not always clear. As Votaw notes:

> The term [social responsibility] is a brilliant one; it means something, but not always the same thing, to everybody. To some it conveys the idea of legal responsibility or liability; to others, it means socially responsible *behavior* in an ethical sense; to still others, the meaning transmitted is that of "responsible for," in a causal mode; many simply equate it with a charitable contribution; some take it to mean socially conscious; many of those who embrace it most fervently see it as a mere synonym for "legitimacy," in the context of "belonging" or being proper or valid; a few see it as a sort of fiduciary duty imposing higher standards of behavior on businessmen than on citizens at large. Even the antonyms, socially "irresponsible" and "non-responsible," are subject to multiple interpretations.[8]

In the face of the large number of different, and not always consistent, usages, we restrict our own use of the term *social responsibility* to refer only to a vague and highly generalized sense of social concern that appears to underlie a wide variety of *ad hoc* managerial policies and practices. Most of these attitudes and activities are well-intentioned and even beneficent; few are patently harmful. They lack, however, any coherent relationship to the managerial unit's internal activities or to its fundamental linkage with its host environment. By contrast, our own term *public responsibility* is

---

[8]Dow Votaw, "Genius Becomes Rare," in Votaw and Sethi, *The Corporate Dilemma*, p. 11. The earliest use of the term *responsibility* in this context appears to have been by J.M. Clark in "The Changing Basis of Economic Responsibility," *Journal of Political Economy*, XXIV (March, 1916), pp. 209-29. Clark concluded, perhaps too optimistically, "that business responsibility beyond the law is not an ideal only but to a considerable extent a fact. . . . All that is needed is to make it cover a larger group—to make it general" (p. 227).

intended to define the functions of organizational management within the specific context of public policy. The "corporate dilemma" can be stated as the problem of defining the specific limits and consequences of managerial social involvement in a particular situation and deciding what—if anything—to do about them. The principle of public responsibility is intended to provide a source of specific and concrete answers to that problem.

The actual involvement of a particular managerial unit with the rest of society can be described in terms of a central core of relationships falling within its area of *primary involvement* and a larger and more varied set of *secondary or consequential involvements.* Within the area of primary involvement for a particular firm are all those relationships with the rest of society that arise directly from its specialized functional role. Most of these relationships will take the form of exchange transactions, either to gain access to factors of production or to transfer goods and services to subsequent users. In addition, relationships with government involving taxation, land use, operating permission, and so on, associated with the role-specialized tasks are also included. All of these areas are *primary* because they are intrinsic to the character of the managerial unit itself in its social context. Without them, the organization cannot be what it is. They create *involvement* because they require interaction between the organization and some other elements of society. Hence, the *area of primary involvement* constitutes the core of relationships between the unit and its social environment.

Beyond this core of relationships there are impacts and effects not intrinsic to the character of the organization but generated by its primary involvement activities. These consequential and derivative relationships define the *area of secondary involvement.* Primary and secondary involvement areas are not sharply distinguished in all cases; one shades into the other. This presents no difficulty for our analysis since there is no distinction between the two in terms of social importance or order of priority. The primary activities define the organization and distinguish it from others; secondary involvements may be similar among a number of quite different organizations. Yet the secondary impacts may be fully as significant, both for internal management and for society at large, as the primary activities in all instances.

We specifically avoid here any reference to a distinction between "commercial products" as opposed to "social products." Although most activities associated with the "commercial products" of a firm fall within its primary involvement area, other relationships—again, taxation, for example—also within this area are not "commercial" in any strict sense. Further, many of the problems and relationships arising out of secondary involvements (e.g., product safety in final use) are essentially "commercial," or at least "economic." We shall argue below that the areas of primary and secondary involvement of the managerial unit define the scope of its responsibility in society, and that other aspects of society—however historically significant or morally praiseworthy they may be—fall outside of its managerial purview.

Public Policy

An effective short definition of the word *policy* is *principles guiding action.* This definition stresses the idea of generality—*principles* rather than specific rules, programs, practices, or the actions themselves. It also emphasizes activity or behavior, as opposed to passive adherence. The idea is that actions are undertaken to accomplish objectives and that both the objectives themselves and the activities suitable for their accomplishment are embraced by the term *policy.*

Public policy—the principles that guide action relating to society as a whole—may be made explicit in law and other formal acts of governmental bodies, but a narrow and legalistic interpretation of the term *policy* should be avoided. Implicit policies—policies that can be implemented without formal articulation of individual actions and decisions—may be even more important. At the same time, *policy* is a more precise and formal concept than mere public opinion, attitude, or belief. These latter forces, when sharply defined and powerfully represented, may bring about changes in public policy itself; more frequently, they reflect recognition of policy goals already established and implemented.

The collection of topics and issues with respect to which public policy may be formulated is referred to as the public policy *agenda.* National defense is on the public policy agenda in most developed societies; styles of dress generally are not. The prohibition of public policy in some areas—such as in the practice of religion in the U.S.—is, of course, itself a matter of public policy.

The nature of public policy, the distinction between policy and law, and the fact that both the issues on the policy agenda and the specific content of policy with respects to particular issues are subject to change over time, may be illustrated with some examples.

Public policy in the United States does not tolerate human slavery, although it once did so. It provides that serious and expensive efforts be made to prevent homicides and to capture and punish murderers. By contrast, other formally illegal activities—petty theft, prostitution, and child abuse, for example—are widely tolerated. It is not, in general, public policy to incur costs or invade privacy sufficiently to eliminate these practices. Another example that emphasizes the distinction between policy and law is the regular waxing and waning of efforts to control gambling in most large cities. These fluctuations usually reflect policy changes with respect to interpretation and enforcement, not changes in the formal content of law itself.

With more specific reference to the economic life, the dominant public policy in the U.S. has favored private ownership of economic resources and private control of the production, distribution, and pricing of goods and services. The modern corporation is, in fact, a social invention designed to permit the combination of private ownership interests into economic units larger or more risky than any single owner could undertake. The general policy that most economic activity will be conducted under private auspices is, however, nowhere explicitly stated in American law, and is revealed most clearly by the specific exceptions to this policy that have been from time to time enacted.

With respect to labor services, an initial policy favoring individual contracting between employer and employee has given way to one of formal support of private labor organizations, including not only their right of collective bargaining but also their power to discipline their own members (by denial of access to employment, for example). Other classic examples of the reversal of the content of public policy with respect to particular social issues are the switch from Jim Crow laws to integrationist policies in race relations and nationwide prohibition of the sale of alcoholic beverages, subsequently followed by repeal.

Congressional enactments declare "restraint of trade" to be illegal and firmly endorse the goal of "maximum employment, production, and purchasing power"; yet public policy has in fact permitted, and often encouraged, significant departures for both market competition and full employment. In these and many other examples we can state with some generality the specific differences among public policy, statute law, and popular opinion.

Perhaps the most important and far-reaching aspects of public policy development are the changes that gradually take place in the policy agenda itself. An historic agenda item now largely forgotten is the protection of the civilian population from mistreatment by military establishment. The Third Amendment to the Constitution, which limits the quartering of soldiers in private houses, reflects the high priority once given to this issue. A recent addition to the policy agenda is the issue of society-wide health and medical care availability and standards, matters formerly left to personal decision and action.

To conclude, public policy reflects general societal commitments and shared values. It incorporates both social goals and the means of accomplishing them. It is responsive to, and reflected in, both public opinion and formal law, yet can differ from each in highly significant ways.

SUMMARY

This chapter introduces our basic thesis that there is an inherently interactive and symbiotic relationship between the private business organization and the larger society that constitutes its host environment. This relationship has been subject to considerable discussion and analysis for the past two decades and to general consideration and comment for a much longer period. At the present time—and in spite of the strong views of a few dissenters—the idea that private management is expected to take into account certain aspects of its broader social involvement seems to be widely accepted.

However, previous analyses provide neither a clear basis for defining the appropriate scope of managerial responsibility nor an explanation of the mechanism through which the goals and objectives of social involvement are to be determined. The thesis of this book is that the scope of managerial responsibility can be defined in terms of a comprehensive model of the management-society relationship, and the goals to be served—which then become criteria for appraising the managerial unit's social performance—are determined through the public policy process, as well as the market mechanism.

CHAPTER TWO

Models of Management
and Society

Models of Social Systems
The Legal Model
The Market Contract Model
The Exploitation Model
The Technostructure Model
An Interpenetrating Systems Model
Summary

In the preceding chapter we referred to managerial organizations as micro-units or subsystems within a larger society, and to society as a whole as a large and complex macro-system, containing numerous components and subsystems within it. In this chapter we extend these references to systems theory in order to describe and contrast some fundamental conceptions of the functional relationship between individual managerial units and their host environment.

We refer to these conceptions as "models" because they are highly simplified and brief sketches of very complex and even obscure relationships; yet such models can be useful as means of describing and contrasting critical viewpoints. For example, if one thinks of the private business enterprise primarily in terms of a *legal* model of the firm, certain basic characteristics, limitations, and roles immediately come to mind. If one thinks of it primarily in *economic* terms, another group of features is suggested. And when the firm is viewed as a *social* institution, still another set of relationships becomes paramount. No one of these conceptions is necessarily more complete or correct than another; and none of them *alone* provides a comprehensive basis for the analysis. Yet each may be appropriately used for certain purposes, without reference to the others, and all may be combined if a comprehensive analysis is required.

Our analysis begins with a presentation of the *legal model* of the private business organization within our society. This conception is of intrinsic importance; moreover, it emphasizes the fact that the fundamental existence of managerial units as we know them rests upon their acceptance by society and, in the case of corporations, their specific authorization in public policy. The remainder of the chapter presents several fundamental and sharply contrasting conceptual models in which the legal, economic, and social characteristics of micro-units are combined and emphasized in various ways. The *market contract model,* familiar from traditional economic and political theory, is contrasted with its classic opposite, the Marxian model of *exploitation.* These two historic conceptions—which, upon examination, turn out to have some important features in common—are shown to be quite distinct in both assumptions and implications from the now-popular idea of a "managed society," as suggested by the *technostructure model* based on the analyses of Burnham and Galbraith. Finally, elements from these several prior models are combined into our own synthetic model, which is based on the concept of *interpenetrating systems.*

MODELS OF SOCIAL SYSTEMS

A *system* consists of two or more components or subsystems that interact with each other and that are separated from their larger environment by a boundary. Systems that are completely self-contained, involving no interactions with the environment, are described as "closed." Although a pure closed system is only a theoretical possibility, the degree to which a system is closed or open provides an important basis for analysis. Any "open" system—which includes any system that can be actually observed—is involved in some sort of transformation of inputs received from the larger environment into outputs discharged into that environment. The boundary of the system filters the type or kinds of inputs that the system can receive from the environment and the outputs that can be discharged. The boundary also determines the time rate of flow of input and output between the system and its environment. This general system conception is, of course, now widely used throughout the physical, biological, and social sciences.[1]

Social systems are invariably "open" and involve the exchange of inputs

[1] Classic references to general systems theory include: K.E. Boulding, "Toward A General Theory of Growth," *General Systems Yearbook I,* (1956), 66-75; E. Nagel, *The Structure of Science* (New York: Harcourt, Brace, 1961); L. Von Bertalanffy, "An Outline of General System Theory," *British Journal of Philosophical Science* (1950), I, 134-65; and L. Von Bertalanffy and A. Rappaport, eds., *The General Systems Yearbook* (Ann Arbor, Mich.: Society for General Systems Research, 1956), annual editions. Our own orientation and terminology is derived from F. Kenneth Berrien, *General and Social Systems* (New Brunswick, N.J.: Rutgers University Press, 1968).

and outputs with the larger environment. Some individual social systems may be extremely and continuously open—with many different types of inputs and outputs crossing their boundaries at all times—while others are relatively closed or only periodically engaged in interactions with the environment. A household of family members intimately involved in the life of its local community is an example of an extremely open micro-system, a small subsystem functioning within the larger social framework. The same family living in a remote location and with infrequent and highly specialized contacts with the outside world might constitute a system almost closed.

Large elements of the social environment—communities, industries, regions, and so on—and even society itself are described as macro-systems or *suprasystems,* involving numerous large and complex subsystems as internal components. Some macro-systems exist only through the independent interactions of their subsystem components and without any overall locus of direction or control. *Dominant suprasystems,* however, are those which, once developed, take on an independent existence and exert a degree of control over their internal components. The national economy of the United States is a suprasystem in which central control or dominance is almost entirely lacking; even the economy-wide impact of federal government activity is only one among many influences at work within the aggregate. By contrast, a centrally planned economy is a dominant suprasystem; the overall plan is used to guide the activities of the subsystem components. Our own federal government could also be described as a dominant suprasystem originally formed through the interaction of the component (subsystem) states.

Systems are said to be *interpenetrating* when more than one distinct system, neither totally contained by nor containing the other, is involved in a single event or process. As Parsons states: "Where it is necessary to speak of two or more analytically distinguishable relational systems as *both* constituting partial determinants of process in a concrete empirical system, we speak of the systems as *interpenetrating.*"[2]

Our own analysis of the management-society relationship is cast in terms of this interpenetrating systems concept. Therefore, we wish to distinguish as sharply as possibly between an *interpenetrating systems model,* in which two separate systems determine a single process, and two more familiar conceptions: *collateral systems models,* in which two or more systems are engaged in transformation and exchange relationships with each other; and *suprasystems models,* in which the activities of subsystems and components are dom-

---

[2]Talcott Parsons, "An Approach to Psychological Theory in Terms of the Theory of Action," in *Psychology: A Study of Science,* ed. Sigmund Koch (New York: McGraw-Hill Book Company, 1959), III, 612-711. Quote from p. 649; italics in original. See also Talcott Parsons, "A Paradigm for the Analysis of Social Systems and Change," in *System, Change, and Conflict,* ed. N.J. Demerath and Richard A Peterson (New York: The Free Press, 1967), pp. 189-212. For an interesting application of this concept, see Raymond G. Hunt and Ira S. Rubin, "Approaches to Managerial Control in Interpenetrating Systems: The Case of Government-Industry Relations," *Academy of Management Journal,* XVI, No. 2 (1973), 296-311.

FIGURE 2-1

Basic Social Systems Model

A: Collateral Systems

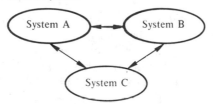

B: Dominant Suprasystem

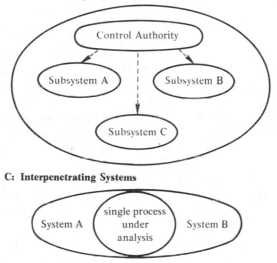

C: Interpenetrating Systems

inated by system-wide authority or influence. These three general classes of models are illustrated in Figure 2-1.

THE LEGAL MODEL

The legal framework of our society is a suprasystem in which the authority of the state is used to preserve a stable and harmonious social order. In some instances—as, for example, with respect to criminal activity—state authority is exercised directly. In others, however, the state merely maintains a system of guidelines and institutions (laws and courts) through which individual parties can engage in collaterial interactions to preserve and pursue their own interests and resist the impositions of others.[3]

[3]See Harold J. Berman and William R. Greiner, *The Nature and Functions of Law,* 3rd ed. (Mineola, N.Y.: The Foundation Press, Inc., 1972), especially Chap. 1.

The status of a business enterprise within the legal framework is a fundamental aspect of its existence. In general, the establishment and growth of private firms has been encouraged by our legal system, although private operations have been prohibited in some areas (not only criminal activity, but also postal service and national defense). At the heart of the relationship between the business firm and the legal system is the concept of *legal entity*. An entity is anything that possesses the quality of oneness and may therefore be regarded as a single unit. A legal entity is any unit recognized in law as having the capacity to possess legal rights and to be subject to legal obligations.[4] A legal entity is thus able to acquire, own, and dispose of property; it can enter contracts, commit wrongs, sue and be sued.

Human beings are legal entities of natural origin, possessing legal capacity and legal status. A proprietorship is such a natural person participating in market transactions as a business on a regular and continuing basis. A proprietorship is thus responsible for meeting all the obligations of a business firm, as well as those of an individual, as prescribed by law. Partnerships are associations of individuals participating in market transactions as a business on a regular and continuing basis. They are generally viewed as not having an independent legal existence apart from their members. Since a partnership is not a legal entity in itself, its obligations and responsibilities are those of the individual partners, each of whom—like the proprietor—is fully responsible both as an individual and as a business firm.

Although proprietorships and partnerships are much more numerous than corporations, the latter are clearly the dominant form of business unit in terms of economic influence. Corporations account for an overwhelming share of the revenues and assets of all business enterprises, and their pervasive importance in our society is even greater than simple numerical measures would indicate. However, each organizational form has certain particular advantages and disadvantages in specific situations; and once a legal form has been adopted by a firm, the form itself may have an important effect on the organization's capacity for and direction of future development. The essential feature of the *corporate form* is that it separates the existence and responsibilities of the organization from those of its individual human participants. Whereas the law simply recognizes and sanctions the existence and economic activity of individuals in the proprietorship and the partnership, the corporation exists as a creation of law.

The development of new forms of business organization and relationships has been described as an aspect of the enlargement of options available to individuals in the pursuit of their individually conceived purposes. Thus, the earlier common-law tradition of agreements and legal associations among individuals enforced by the judiciary gradually gave way to the development of collective organizations on the one hand and to an expanding role for the legislative arm of the state on the other. As Hurst comments: "It was inevi-

---

[4]Len Young Smith and G. Gale Roberson, *Business Law,* 3rd ed. (St. Paul, Minn.: West Publishing Company, 1971), p. 720.

able that the legislature play a larger part in regard to corporation law. It did not lie in judicial power to grant charters, and men saw issues in this field too broad and turbulent to fit within the confines of lawsuits."[5] Thus, the state became the creator of new forms of organization, and widespread adoption of general incorporation statutes has greatly broadened the privilege of corporate form and served to popularize it.

The source of corporate existence is the *charter*. Unlike proprietorships and partnerships, which can arise without the formality of public approval, corporations cannot legally exist without governmental authorization. The chartering process serves to confirm publicly the view that the economic system and the organizations participating in it are performing a social function that is endorsed by society's political arm, the state. Corporate charters are either *restricted* or *general* in their terms. Restricted grants limit the types of activities that the corporation may perform. Thus, hospitals and schools, nonprofit charities, and municipalities are each chartered to perform specific types of activities. Should the grants become outdated or merit modification, resort must be had to the public policy process in order to secure change. General grants, however, rely upon the larger system within which the chartered unit will be participating to stimulate the unit to act in a manner that will prove socially beneficial. General grants are, in effect, licenses for the corporation to act as its management sees fit, the assumption being that management's choice of activities will constitute a rational response to the stimuli generated by society as a whole and hence serve a "social purpose."

THE MARKET CONTRACT MODEL

The expectation that legal business entities will interact with each other so as to reveal and respond to social needs rests on an important historical idea that we shall term the *market contract model*. This model underlies the traditional doctrines of liberal economic and political theory. It is made explicit here so that the similarities and differences of other models to be presented can be clearly indicated and so that it can be referred to in later chapters, particularly in connection with the discussion of "fundamentalism" in Chapter 3.

The essential idea of the market contract model is that each participant in the economy—down to the individual firm, household, and productive worker—obtains its share of the benefits available in society by providing goods and performing services that are desired by other social entities and individuals. The firm or individual makes, in effect, a "market contract" with other members of society, provides them with something they desire on terms more favorable than they can obtain elsewhere, and obtains its own share of the "social product" from them in return. As Adam Smith described

---

[5]James Willard Hurst, *Law and the Conditions of Freedom in the Nineteenth-Century United States* (Madison: University of Wisconsin Press, 1956), p. 15.

the situation: "Every man . . . lives by exchanging, or becomes in some measure a merchant, and the society itself grows to be what is properly called a commercial society."[6]

According to the market contract model, a business firm comes into being because it can perform desired functions for other members of society on favorable terms. If the market will sustain the enterprise, it continues and perhaps thrives. If tastes change, costs rise, or more favorable competitive alternatives appear, it declines and then must find some other functions to perform, or it will simply pass out of existence. Any problems that cannot be resolved by the market test must be referred elsewhere—to the political decision-making system, for example—or left to private social action and charity. Issues of "social involvement" are fully resolved by the basic test that some specific task must be performed on terms that at least some customers are willing to pay.

The pure market contract model is amoral and pragmatic, since, as Adam Smith pointed out: "It is not from the benevolence of the butcher, the brewer, or the baker, that we expect our dinner, but from their regard to their own interest. We address ourselves not to their humanity but to their self-love, and never talk to them of our own necessities but of their advantages. Nobody but a beggar chooses to depend chiefly upon the benevolence of his fellow citizens."[7]

The social philosophy associated with the market contract model is not, however, pessimistic or critical. On the contrary, the interplay of forces of self-interest is thought to lead as if by an "invisible hand" to a harmonious outcome for society as a whole. In the most idealistic version of the analysis, competition assures a close relationship between prices and costs; the accumulation of capital permits mechanization and the division of labor; and increasing productivity results in "the progress of opulence" over time.

Whether or not these conclusions can be fully anticipated, one key feature of the market contract model for present purposes is its assumption of a complete and sharp distinction between each market contracting unit, from the individual worker to the largest enterprise, and all other units and individuals within the system. It is a *collateral systems model* [see Figure 2-1(A)] in which each component entity is isolated from every other one, and interactions take place *only* by means of transactions. This assumed separation and isolation extends even to government itself, which, in the pure market contract analysis, is essentially a subsystem among other subsystems. It performs the key functions of maintaining law and order and providing public services, but its relationship with the other units of society comes down essentially to market exchange. Although Adam Smith himself, and most other writers in the liberal tradition, expressed strong personal views as

[6]Adam Smith, *The Wealth of Nations,* ed. Edwin Cannan (New York: Random House, Inc., 1937), p. 22.

[7]*Ibid.,* p. 14.

to the proper (and improper) role of the political state, the model itself implies that the state should provide such services as the members of society desire, and on terms that they are willing to pay. Social decision making through the political process exists entirely apart from the market contracting system, and the latter is seen as the principal and most desirable form of social coordination and decision making. Any impact of government or other forms of collective social direction on the market contract process and its results can be unambiguously termed "interference."

THE EXPLOITATION MODEL

Diametrically opposed to the market contract model is a conception of the management-society relationship as a system of exploitation. Although this conception has its roots in the Marxian analysis of capitalist exploitation, it is equally applicable to the self-interested social dominance of dictators, commissars, and bureaucrats. (An old socialist joke has it that "Capitalism is the exploitation of man by man; socialism is the reverse.")

In the elementary Marxian exposition, capitalistic production inevitably involves the exploitation of labor by the capitalist (i.e., owner-manager) class. Marx viewed the value of all goods and services as due ultimately to the labor required to produce them. The capitalist hires labor and purchases materials in order to resell the resulting products at prices higher than costs, thus obtaining a profit. His object is not the production process itself (the production of commodities), but only the profit obtained (the production of capital). Each addition to capital increases the ability of the capitalist to employ labor and to expropriate additional "surplus value" (i.e., profit) arising as a result of production; and each round of production and sales increases the stock of capital and hence the capacity for exploitation by the capitalists. "Accumulate accumulate! That is Moses and the prophets!"[8]

The basic exploitation model was subsequently extended by Marx, and even more vigorously by Rosa Luxemburg, to include an emphasis on inter-racial and international relationships, particularly imperialism. "Capital, impelled to appropriate productive forces for purposes of exploitation, ransacks the whole world. . . ."[9] A half-century later an African representative to a conference on multinational corporations declared that a small nation is "virtually at the mercy" of such corporations in their "eminently rational" search for efficiency and profits. "No matter how one looks at it, foreign investment involves exploitation (in the Marxist sense) of the resources of the host country."[10]

[8]Karl Marx, *Capital,* ed. Frederick Engels, trans. Samuel Moore and Edward Aveling (New York: Random House, Inc., 1906), p. 652 (This edition contains one volume only.)

[9]Rosa Luxemburg, *The Accumulation of Capital,* trans. Agnes Schwarzchild (New York: Monthly Review Press, 1964), p. 358.

[10]*Wall Street Journal,* January 29, 1973, p. 1.

In its modern version the *exploitation model* describes any situation in which a dominant social or economic class controls society for the pursuit of its own particular interests, extracting all available socio-economic benefits for use toward those ends. In this sense the exploitation model underlies the common conception of both the nineteenth-century "robber barons" in the U.S. and the political and administrative leaders in Nazi Germany and Stalinist Russia. It also accounts for the attitude, reflected above, of many less-developed host countries toward large international firms operating within their borders. The essential idea is that there are two types of collateral subsystems—exploiting units and exploited units—and that the exploiting units use their dominant power position to extract maximum benefits and thus maintain and enlarge their spheres of special interest.

The elementary Marxian notion of exploitation grew out of—and, indeed, in opposition to—the market contract notions of the classical economists, whose work Marx described as "learned disputation [about] how the booty pumped out of the labourer may be divided, with most advantage to accumulation, between the industrial capitalist and the rich idler. . . ."[11] However, the Marxian analysis shares with the earlier model a basic amorality. Marx viewed "the evolution of the economic formation of society . . . as a process of natural history," in which the individual cannot be held "responsible for relations whose creature he socially remains. . . ."[12] The notion of "social responsibility" (or irresponsibility) as an aspect of private business management would have been as foreign to Marx as to Adam Smith.

In all other respects, however, the Marxian model presents the sharpest possible contrast to the liberal conception of a harmonious society based upon market contract relationships. Where Smith—and liberal economists down to the present—viewed business profits as essentially rewards for successful accomplishment of socially desired tasks and indicators of direction for needed economic expansion, for Marx the rate of profit was synonymous with "the intensity of exploitation." This reversal of relationships replaced the inherent harmony of the classical conception with a system of inherent conflicts and contradictions leading to ultimate collapse. According to the idealized market contract model, an entire economy in which each individual and organization operates on the same (i.e., market contract) economic principle is viable and stable. By contrast, the Marxian model identifies two distinct groups—the exploiters and the exploited—and holds that "capitalism . . . depends in all respects on non-capitalist strata and social organizations existing side by side with it."[13] The capitalist system eventually collapses either because all possible exploitation possibilities are used up or because political and social revolution is brought about by the exploited groups themselves.

[11]Marx, *Capital*, p. 653.
[12]*Ibid.*, p. 15.
[13]Luxemburg, *The Accumulation of Capital*, p. 365.

THE TECHNOSTRUCTURE MODEL

The market contract and exploitation models of the management-society relationship share a second characteristic in addition to the absence of moral and ethical content: They assume a clear and sharp separation between the ownership-control element of each individual managerial unit and the "rest of society" within which that unit operates. For Adam Smith, each economic unit, including the household, exists in isolation and relates to the rest of society through the mechanism of market exchange. Similarly, for Marx, each capitalist unit—and the capitalist class as a whole—is sharply distinguished from the rest of society and relates to it through the process of exploitation.

Both of these collateral systems models contrast sharply with suprasystems models in which society as a whole is shown to be functionally integrated and managed by some dominant control authority or group [see Figure 2-1(B)]. Centralized control by the state would, of course, constitute one form of suprasystem dominance. However, since there seems to be no widespread opinion that such a model would describe our current society, it does not require development here. On the other hand, the now-popular conception of an integrated society consisting primarily of large managerial organizations and dominated by their collective staffs of high-level professionals is a suprasystem model of some significance. Borrowing Galbraith's term, we refer to this conception as the *technostructure model.*

The technostructure model was first developed in Burnham's *The Managerial Revolution* (1941), and was more recently presented in Galbraith's *The New Industrial State* (1967). Both of these authors started with the familiar idea of the separation of ownership and control in the large business enterprise and the associated development of a professional managerial class. They then argued that the elite of the managerial class, whom Galbraith termed "the Technostructure," not only take over individual organizations within society, but these large organizations simultaneously expand and develop interconnections so that the technostructure gradually comes to dominate society as a whole. This domination, however, is not essentially exploitative; neither can it be described in market contract terms. On the contrary, in the process of taking over society, the technostructure comes to be taken over *by* society, embracing social goals and objectives even as it shapes tastes and values through its own behavior. Eventually, the individual manager, the technostructure as a group, the large organization, and society as a whole tend to merge into a single decision-action system in which particularistic goals, efforts, and rewards cannot be readily identified.

As Galbraith describes the process,

> The individual member of the Technostructure identifies himself with the goals of the mature corporation as, and because, the corporation identifies itself with goals which have, or appear to him to have, social purpose.

• • •

It is the genius of the industrial system that it makes the goals that reflect its needs—efficient production of goods, a steady expansion in their output (and) . . . consumption, . . . technological change, autonomy for the technostructure, an adequate supply of trained and educated manpower—coordinate with social virture and human enlightenment.

• • •

Given the deep dependence of the industrial system on the state and . . . . its identification with public goals and the adaptation of these to its needs, the industrial system will not long be regarded as something apart from government. . . . Increasingly it will be recognized that the mature corporation, as it develops, becomes part of the larger administrative complex associated with the state. In time the line between the two will disappear. Men will look back in amusement at the pretense that once caused people to refer to General Dynamics and North American Aviation and AT&T as *private* business.[14]

The Galbraithian vision may yet be rather far from reality in the U.S., and its details correspondingly indistinct. By contrast, a similar technocrat-manager development has frequently been noted to be a characteristic feature of present-day Japan. "Japan Incorporated" has gained unquestioned use as a "description of one of the world's largest economies as though it were a single, coordinated, centrally managed business unit. . . . This relationship is not comparable to that of a socialist economy, with the state in control . . . nor yet analogous to the United States in the late nineteenth century, with government essentially an instrumentality of big business."[15] On the contrary, the similarity of personal goals, training, and experience among Japanese political, economic, and social leaders apparently accounts for the overall harmony and broad social comprehensiveness of their viewpoints.

AN INTERPENETRATING SYSTEMS MODEL

The two classic models of market contract and exploitation contain several important truths. One is that the managerial unit is, to some extent, a

[14]John Kenneth Galbraith, *The New Industrial State* (Boston: Houghton Mifflin Company, 1967), pp. 166, 343, and 393. See also James Burnham, *The Managerial Revolution* (New York: The John Day Company, Inc., 1941). The trend toward a managerial (rather than purely capitalist) society had been earlier detected by Marx, who should perhaps be viewed as the precursor of Berle and Means (*The Modern Corporation and Private Property,* 1932) as well as Burnham and Galbraith. Citing a now-forgotten "Mr. Ure," Marx states that "the industrial managers, and not the industrial capitalists, are 'the soul of our industrial system' . . . The labour of superintendence, entirely separated from the ownership of capital, walks the streets. . . . It is private production without the control of private property." Karl Marx and Friedrich Engels, *Capital,* III, (Chicago: Charles H. Kerr & Company, 1906), pp. 454-5.

[15]James C. Abegglen, "Japan, Incorporated: Government and Business as Partners," in *Changing Market Systems . . . Consumer, Corporate and Government Interfaces,* 1967 Winter Conference Proceedings Series, No. 26 (Washington, D.C.: American Marketing Association, December 27-29, 1967), pp. 228-32. Quote from p. 228. See also Eugene J. Kaplan, *Japan: The Government-Business Relationship* (Washington, D.C.: U.S. Department of Commerce, February 1972). A sharp contrast is provided by the recent *America, Inc.,* which takes an essentially exploitation-model view of business, political, and media leadership in our own society. See Morton Mintz and Jerry S. Cohen, *America, Inc.* (New York: Dial Press, 1971), paperback ed.

distinct element within society, not simply an operating mechanism within some larger rationalized and controlled system. Another is that there are elements of *quid pro quo* (exchange), as well as elements of power and advantage (exploitation), in most important social relationships. At the same time, the extreme separation of the managerial unit from the "rest of society," whether for purposes of pure exchange or unfettered exploitation, required in these models contrasts too sharply with common experience reflecting cohesiveness and a broad commonality of interest—and hence bases for cooperation rather than conflict—along social entities. On the other hand, the full-blown technostructure model appears to overstate both the integration and the rationality of social relationships and to underestimate the importance of pluralism, adaptability, initiative, and innovation. Hence, we present here a synthetic model, less precise than any of those previously discussed, although admitting all of them—as well as many other variations and combinations—as special cases.

Our model is based on the concept of *interpenetrating systems* [see Figure 2-1(C)]. We assume that the larger society exists as a macro-system, but that individual (and particularly *large*) micro-organizations also constitute separable systems within themselves, neither completely controlling nor controlled by the social environment. As Cohen and Cyert describe the situation, "The organization and the environment are parts of a complex interactive system. The actions taken by the organization can have important effects on the environment, and, conversely, the outcomes of the actions of the organization are partially determined by events in the environment. These outcomes and the events that contribute to them have a major impact on the organization. Even if the organization does not respond to these events, significant changes in the organizational participants' goals and roles can occur."[16]

To illustrate the interpenetrating system concept, assume that some firm—an independent entrepreneur or one already organized—decides to pursue a particular path of technological research and development. The firm will draw information and resources—as well as ideas about commercially useful development paths—from the larger society. But the larger society will not in any concrete or conscious way control the development paths pursued—neither their direction nor their success. The development project may yield only trivial results, or none at all. On the other hand, it may yield an innovation comparable to the automobile, the computer, or the electric lamp. In the latter case, the firm does not simply "exchange" the resulting product in a collateral relationship with the rest of society—neither does it do so on a harmonious market contract basis nor in

[16]Kalman J. Cohen and Richard M. Cyert, "Strategy: Formulation, Implementation, and Monitoring," *The Journal of Business* XLVI, No. 3 (1973), 352. See also, Paul R. Lawrence and Jay W. Lorsch, *Organization and Environment: Managing Differentiation and Integration* (Boston: Division of Research, Graduate School of Business Administration, Harvard University, 1967); Neil W. Chamberlain, *Enterprise and Environment* (New York: McGraw-Hill Book Company, 1968); and J. David Singer, *A General Taxonomy for Political Science* (New York: General Learning Press, 1971).

order to expropriate the surplus value. On the contrary, the introduction of the innovation by the micro-unit generates both new flows of activity and substantial structural changes within the macro-system itself. It is this ability of one system to change the *structure* of the other, and not simply to alter the volume or character of inputs and outputs, that distinguishes the interpenetrating systems model from simpler collateral or suprasystems conceptions.

The interpenetrating systems model also facilitates the analysis of the changing role of society, as expressed through formal public policy, *vis-à-vis* the managerial organization. In the market contract model, the state itself is merely one among many separate system units, collecting taxes and tolls in return for services rendered. However, the development of social concern for working conditions, culminating in public policy actions to limit the hours of work or provide protection for health and safety, cannot be described in market contract (still less in exploitation) terms. On the contrary, we require a model that permits society to influence and constrain—but not necessarily dominate or control—an area of activity formerly reserved to the firm exclusively. Similarly, attempts by individual organizations to affect the course of public policy—whether by bribery or persuasion—may be described as an expansion of managerial activity into the decision system of society at large. In neither example does one system necessarily come to control the other completely, even with respect to the specific matter involved and certainly not in *all* matters. Nor can the relationship between the systems be described in the simple terms of input-output or exchange. On the contrary, the concept of interpenetration seems to be, if less precise, the more accurate general form of the relationship between micro-organizational management and its social environment.

An interpenetrating systems model opens up the possibility—which has, in fact, become a necessity—of considering the potential differences, conflicts, and compatabilities among the goals of micro-organizations and those of society at large. In both the market contract and exploitation models it is assumed that organizations are responsive to their own individual goals and that these goals are balanced (favorably or unfavorably) with those of other system components through the exchange process. In the fully developed technostructure model there can be no goal disharmony; the goals of the managerial class and those of industrial society as a whole have, through the process of adoption and adaptation, become the same. By contrast, the interpenetrating systems model can accommodate both the separateness and possible conflict of managerial and societal goals on one hand and the process of managerial/societal goal adjustment on the other. Society may take into account and seek to influence the goals of the managerial units; and they, in turn, may take into account and seek to influence those of society at large. Neither are the two systems completely separate and independent nor does either control the other; their relationship is better described in terms of interpenetration. As Virgil B. Day, vice-president of General Electric, has remarked:

> The social and economic responsibilities of the corporation have been so broadened and interwoven in the public's expectations . . . that it no longer makes sense, if, indeed, it ever did, to talk as if they could be separated.[17]
>
> • • •
>
> . . . [E]very corporation has not only a legal charter, that is, the charter of public expectations of corporate performance. These expectations derive from the current set of social values and national goals; and, as these values and goals change so too will the social charter of the corporation.[18]

SUMMARY

This chapter began with the presentation of some basic terms and concepts from general systems theory that were then used to delineate five theoretical models of the relationship between business organizations and their social environment.

In the legal model the individual firm exists as a subsystem within the suprasystem of the legal framework of society. Legal entities, particularly corporations, exist specifically as a result of social decisions and public policy. The legal status of such units reflects a social acceptance of their basic purposes and functional roles. Once this status is accorded, their rights and responsibilities—and their range of discretionary behavior—are defined by the suprasystem itself.

The two comprehensive classic models of the relationship between micro-unit management and the social environment are based on the diametrically opposed concepts of market contract and exploitation. Both of these models may be visualized as collateral systems. They assume that there is a distinct separation between the individual managerial unit and the society in which it exists. This separation can be bridged by mutually satisfactory exchange relationships, as in the market contract model, or by the exploitation of disadvantaged groups for the benefit of an ownership-management class, as in the Marxian analysis. An alternative and newer conception, the technostructure model, assumes that the managerial class controls and is, in turn, controlled by society, so that no sharp separation or disharmony of interests can exist. In essence, society as a whole is "managed" by the technostructure, but the goals of the managers and of society as a whole have become identical.

[17]Virgil B. Day, "Management and Society: An Insider's View," *Management and Public Policy* (Proceedings of a Conference, School of Management, State University of New York at Buffalo, September 1971), pp. 155-75.

[18]Virgil B. Day, "Business Priorities in a Changing Environment," *Journal of General Management*, I, No. 1 (1973), p. 48.

Although each of these familiar conceptions captures certain key features of reality, each is deficient in certain respects as a basis for analysis and interpretation of our own society. Therefore, we have suggested a model of interpenetrating systems, which assumes neither complete integration nor complete separation between micro-managerial units and their larger host environment. This model permits the analysis of both conflict and harmony, and of structural adaptation of the two systems to each other over time. The interpenetrating systems model is the core concept of management-society relationships used throughout the remainder of the book and is integrated with a more comprehensive model of the public policy process in Chapter 6.

CHAPTER THREE

The Scope
of Managerial Responsibility:
Fundamentalism

In this and the following chapters, we examine and contrast divergent views as to the appropriate scope of managerial involvement and interaction with the larger social environment. One view, which we term *fundamentalism,* essentially holds that managerial responsibility extends only to those activities required to accomplish the firm's primary tasks and that market transactions serve as the sole criterion of social evaluation, success, or failure. The opposite extreme view, reflected in a good deal of current commentary, is that business management is in some sense responsible for virtually every aspect of social and political—as well as economic—life in our society. Our concept of *public responsibility,* presented in detail in Chapter 7, represents an attempt to establish a middle ground between these extremes. However, the essential fundamentalist position and the several different proposals for departures from it deserve careful consideration on their own merits.

FUNDAMENTALISM

The fundamentalist position is based specifically on the market contract model of management and society relationships, presented in Chapter 2. Fundamentalism accepts the market contract model both as a description of actual relationships within society and as a desirable form of social and economic coordination. According to the market contract model, each unit (firm or individual) in society makes an implicit market contract with the other members of society, providing them with goods and services they desire on terms more favorable than they can obtain elsewhere and obtaining its own requirements and rewards from them in return. The heart of the fundamentalist case is that the responsiveness of individuals and micro-managerial units to market stimuli throughout society will both *define* the optimal use and distribution of resources and permit that optimal use and distribution be achieved. Hence, managerial involvement in society should be confined to the identification of and response to stimuli arising from markets. Effective discharge of these responsibilities by individuals and managers throughout the system results in the attainment of the most highly desired—and therefore the most desirable—combinations and levels of performance for the system as a whole.

There is some debate as to whether or not the apparent widespread acceptance of fundamentalism, particularly within the business community, is merely a rhetorical façade. On one hand, some analyses suggest that the fundamentalist position, in various forms, is generally understood and strongly endorsed.[1]   Other and more recent observers have drawn a sharp contrast between the conventional rhetoric of capitalism—which may amount to an unintended self-caricature—and the actual and effective views of leading executives. As John R. Bunting describes the situation,

> The businessman has come to be freed from the automatic discipline imposed by the "invisible hand" of competition. . . . Yet, by the very nature of the business system in which he believes, he feels that he must go on attempting to escape discipline. . . . He finds it difficult to imagine that society will permit him to discipline himself if the marketplace can no longer do the whole job. . . . So he protests loudly that what has happened hasn't happened really. Inevitably, however, his actions and his beliefs are adding up to a new kind of system. . . . He is, without acknowledging it, trying to improvise a hand of accepted procedure to replace the familiar invisible hand of competition.[2]

[1]Francis X. Sutton, Seymour E. Harris, Carl Kaysen, and James Tobin, *The American Business Creed* (Cambridge, Mass.; Harvard University Press, 1956).

[2]John R. Bunting, *The Hidden Face of Free Enterprise* (New York: McGraw-Hill Book Company, 1964), pp. 9-10.

In this chapter we summarize these essential arguments in support of the fundamentalist position and then present a short critique. The critique is continued into the following chapter in which several alternatives to the fundamentalist viewpoint are considered in more detail.[3] Whatever the source and strength of support for the fundamentalist position, it can be defended on three grounds. The first and central argument is the positive case for fundamentalism based upon its consistency with the achievement of the social optimum in the context of the market contract model. The second defense is essentially legalistic; it is argued that the legal status of managerial units—specifically corporations—limits their authority to consider or modify the nonmarket aspects of their activities. Finally, fundamentalism is defended through the criticism of its alternatives, criticism that ranges beyond the limits of any particular abstract model of the management-society relationships, and includes social and political considerations as well.

The Positive Argument

The positive case for fundamentalism rests on the concept of role specialization, both within and between micro-organizations, and on the market contract as the device for coordinating activity among role-specialized individuals and groups. To recapitulate briefly: Each individual must perform some useful function within society in order to obtain some portion of goods and services for his own use. If groups of individuals can perform particular functions more efficiently than single persons working alone, organizations come into being. And, as these organizations increase in size and complexity, the specialized function of management evolves. Yet the role of management is confined to the direction and coordination required for the role-specialized task that each particular micro-organization performs in order to engage in exchange transactions with the rest of society. Management can modify or change the task, if it appears in the best interest of the organization to do so. However, according to fundamentalists, what management cannot and should not do is expand the scope of its activities beyond those functions necessary to the successful accomplishment of the task itself, including execution of the resulting transactions. If each individual and organization seeks to accomplish in the most efficient manner the highest-valued specific tasks of which he (it) is capable, the value of the total product of society will be as great as possible. Further, of course, if

[3] The most forceful brief statement of the Fundamentalist position is found in Milton Friedman, "The Social Responsibility of Business Is to Increase Its Profits," *New York Times Magazine,* September 13, 1970. See also "Milton Friedman Responds," *Business and Society Review* No. 1, (Spring 1972), p. 5; Eugene W. Rostow, "To Whom and For What Ends Is Corporate Management Responsible?" (Chapter 3) in *The Corporation in Modern Society,* ed. Edward S. Mason (Cambridge, Mass.: Harvard University Press, 1959), pp. 46-71; Gordon C. Bjork, *Private Enterprise and Public Interest* (Englewood Cliffs, N.J.: Prentice-Hall, Inc., 1969); and Neil W. Chamberlain, *The Limits of Corporate Responsibility* (New York: Basic Books, Inc., 1973).

multiple individuals and organizations vie for the privilege of performing highly valued tasks, competition among them will yield the lowest possible costs, both to themselves and to society at large.

According to the fundamentalist view, any call for broadened social concern on the part of business management is simply a sign that the organizational structure and coordinating mechanism of the economy is deteriorating. Appropriate corrective action is not the imposition of additional nonmarket responsibilities on management but rather a strengthening of market pressures themselves. For example, it is sometimes argued that increasing the power of corporate stockholders would lead to increased managerial emphasis on market penalties and rewards.[4] Insulation from both market pressures and owner interests—and hence insulation against the very forces most likely to press the firm toward economic efficiency—appears to be an essential prerequisite of broadened managerial responsibility. Hence, according to the fundamentalists, the demand for broadened responsibility may carry with it a hidden tendency toward decreased efficiency and further misallocation of resources.

The role of social rewards in excess of costs—or, loosely, "profits"—in the market contract model, and hence in the fundamentalist market position, is worth re-emphasis. Abnormal profits, high wages, and other unusual rewards are evidences that an individual or organization is performing a task that society particularly values. The willingness of society to provide unusually high rewards for particular services should attract additional effort to them, and therefore lead to an expansion in the quantity of them available and a corresponding decline in the (excessive) rewards that they receive. The appearance of abnormal profits and other economic rewards is thus, from the fundamentalist perspective, a necessary and desirable phenomenon, indicating that an organization has been particularly successful in accomplishing social objectives. Hence, as Professor Friedman argues, "The social responsibility of business is to increase its profits."

A second and somewhat subsidiary aspect of the positive case for fundamentalism is its alleged compatibility with political freedom and social pluralism.[5] The argument is essentially that vigorous pursuit of economic objectives by individuals and micro-organizations tends to generate multiple centers of economic and social power, as well as multiple avenues for the development of innovations, so that opportunities for political diversity are maintained, and social structures are altered and revitalized. This social-

---

[4] Frederick Hayek, "The Corporation in a Democratic Society," in *Management and Corporations, 1985,* ed. Melvin Anshen and George Bach (New York: McGraw-Hill Book Company, 1960), p. 116.

[5] This is the theme of Friedman's *Capitalism and Freedom* (Chicago: University of Chicago Press, 1963). Other expressions of this view are found in Joseph A. Schumpeter, *Capitalism, Socialism and Democracy* 3rd ed. (New York: Harper & Row, Publishers, Inc., 1950), and Frederick Hayek, *The Road to Serfdom* (Chicago: University of Chicago Press, 1944).

political proposition, like the basic economic analysis underlying it, rests on a number of strong assumptions about the initial distribution of wealth and power in society, the genuine openness of the market contract economy to new ideas and endeavors, and the strength of tendencies toward the concentration of economic and social power within a market contract society over time. These issues are examined in the following critiques.

The Legal Argument

The legal defense of fundamentalism is based, first, on the concept of the corporate charter as a *limitation* on the scope of business activity and, secondarily, on the legal responsibilities of professional managers with the corporation itself. (The essential argument applies to both corporate and noncorporate business entities, since noncorporate forms receive implicitly the same type of recognition and authority from society that the corporation receives explicitly in its charter.) In Chapter 2, a distinction was drawn between *restricted* grants of corporate authority for particular purposes and *general* grants or charters which authorize a broad or unspecified range of activities. It was pointed out that the notion of general grants presupposes the existence of some system of relationships that will stimulate, direct, and limit the activities of chartered organizations in pursuit of their goals. The matrix of market transactions within which the corporation operates constitutes such as system, but this system provides direction and correction only with respect to its market-related activities. Hence, according to the fundamentalist view, the general grant of corporate authority assumes that the grantee will restrict the scope of its decision making to those spheres of activity within which the market system provides a mechanism for social evaluations, rewards, and penalties. Any expansion of the corporation's sphere of responsibility beyond its area of primary involvement, as defined by the scope of its market transactions, is thus a violation of the implicit terms of its charter.

Within this conception of the legal authority of micro-organizations, the specialized role of the professional manager is clearly defined. The corporate manager serves as an employee and agent of the shareholders, and his task is to accomplish *their* purpose as effectively as possible. This means that he must concentrate on the economic functions for which the organization was established in order to bring about the maximum increase in the value of the organization that has been entrusted to his charge. Any modification of economically optimal plans in the pursuit of additional goals, or the substitution of the objectives of other members of society for those of the stockholders themselves, amounts to malfeasance, comparable to deliberate mismanagement or the misappropriation of funds. According to the fundamentalist view, the introduction of any type of "social" concern is particularly dangerous. Since the market provides no specific test of the validity of such concerns, the manager is inevitably led to base his decisions and activities on his own personal viewpoint and values. The result is that he substitutes his own goals and evaluations for the stimuli and rewards provided by both the market and the shareholders. This in turn undermines his own legitimate authority as an employee and agent, as well as the fundamental legal basis for the existence of the corporation itself.

Appraisal of Alternatives

The third major defense of the fundamentalist position consists of a critique of selected aspects of various alternative proposals. There are four essential themes, two of which are the obverse of the economic and legal arguments just presented.

Loss of Economic Efficiency

If, in fact, the scope of corporate responsibility is expanded beyond the traditional economic framework, corporate managers must modify their behavior in some fashion. And if their unmodified behavior was, in fact, "efficient" in terms of the costs, prices, and technology available, any modification must result in some loss of efficiency. For example, cooperating with inflation-control policies by resisting price increases, and installing pollution controls more powerful and costly than the minimum legal requirements, are clearly "inefficient" activities in the sense that they yield lower profits than would otherwise be obtained. That these actions may be socially useful is not argued. However, they involve the sacrifice of "efficiency" as indicated by market rewards and penalties.

Managerial Incompetence

The very notion of managerial specialization and technical competence in carrying out the functions essential to the corporation's primary task suggests a probable corollary: that successful business managers may have no specific competence—or, indeed, may be particularly incompetent—in identifying and serving other needs of society. If this is the case, even if broader social concerns could be brought within the purview of management without loss of economic efficiency, it is not likely that social goals would be correctly identified or that efficiency would be accomplished.

Essentially, the fundamentalist position states that there is nothing in the set of qualifications and experiences required to attain a position of significant corporate managerial responsibility that is also likely to yield special insight as to the "public interest" in any particular area, nor is special skill acquired in attaining such interests, even if they are properly identified. On the contrary, placing a burden of nonmarket responsibilities on the corporate manager forces him to abandon his professional competence in pursuit of a set of skills that he does not possess and to substitute his personal judgment for that of the public at large.

As Friedman has argued, under these circumstances an expanded scope of corporate responsibility is ". . . a fundamentally subversive doctrine. If businessmen do have a social responsibility other than maximizing profits for stockholders, how are they to know what it is? Can self-selected private individuals decide what burden they are justified in placing on themselves and their stockholders to serve that social interest? Is it tolerable that these public functions of taxation, expenditure, and control be exercised by the people who happen at the moment to be in charge of particular enterprises, chosen for those posts by strictly private groups?"[6]

The incompetence argument does not, of course, challenge for a moment the right or responsibility of the individual executive, stockholder, or employee to participate actively in political or social life and to express his personal views as to the nature of the "public interest" and the means of attaining it. On the contrary, fundamentalists argue merely that authority and power within the managerial structure of micro-organizations should not be uncritically expanded to become authority and power within society at large.

Loss of Political Legitimacy

As previously emphasized, the historic character of the corporation has been that of a private legal entity, created and authorized by the state to undertake certain types of activity. The traditional concept of corporate legitimacy is intimately connected with the idea of private property. When managers divert corporate property into any activity other than furthering the economic interests of the corporation's owners, they are in a sense depriving the owners of their property and thereby weakening the justification both for their own authority and for the existence of the organization itself.

Further, any attempt to transform the corporation into a more public institution, one governed by political processes and acting on some concept of the "public interest," only serves to raise additional questions about its basic legitimacy. Henry Manne, among others, has condemned such attempts, noting that "political notions like shareholder democracy, constituent boards of directors and public interest proxy fights suggest to the unsophisticated that corporations are something like governments, and that shareholders are like citizens born into a particular sovereign regime." The result is a false perception of the corporation, as a "social trusteeship," with a public, rather than private character.[7]

---

[6] Milton Friedman, *Capitalism and Freedom* (Chicago: University of Chicago Press, 1963), pp. 133-34.

[7] Henry G. Manne, "Who's Responsible?" *Barron's*, May 17, 1971, p. 14. Also, Henry G. Manne and Henry C. Wallich, *The Modern Corporation and Social Responsibility* (Washington, D.C.: American Enterprise Institute for Public Policy Research, 1972).

The notion of public trusteeship undermines the legal basis for the private micro-organization in two different ways. First, it expands the scope of corporate responsibility so that the basis of evaluation provided by the market mechanism is invalidated. As a result, one cannot tell whether corporations are acting within or outside their legitimate authority, whether their social performance is improving or deteriorating. Second, the evolution of a political governance system within the organization inevitably leads to a new concept of ownership, control, and management, and hence to the abandonment of the traditional legal concept of the corporate entity itself. Resort to a political mechanism transforms the corporation from a voluntary arrangement into a potentially coercive institution. Such a transformation is not within the legitimate scope of corporate activity and therefore cannot fail to result in a loss—or at least a substantial change—of its political and legal status. Again, it is not necessary to argue that these developments are undesirable—although fundamentalists would do so. Rather, the analytical point is simply that an expansion of a corporation's responsibility beyond the market contract test leads directly to the destruction of its legitimacy as a social institution.

Threat to Social and Political Pluralism

Even if managerial organizations could expand the scope of their responsibilities without excessive loss of economic efficiency, without becoming involved in tasks for which they are totally incompetent, and without undermining their legal status, one final issue remains. Fundamentalists insist that the growth of large and socially involved corporate entities, each with its own broad range of activities and each inevitably intertwined with other similar units and with the state itself, consitutes a threat to social and political pluralism and freedom throughout society.

According to the fundamentalists, two different patterns of development might be anticipated, either of them leading to the same inevitable end. One possibility is that if the market mechanism no longer directs or governs many of the activities of micro-unit management, political direction through the state will become increasingly necessary. The result will be a gradual expansion of centralization and social control, leading eventually to nationalization. The alternative scenario is that the performance of an ever-widening range of public functions will eventually cause corporations to become the principal governance structure of society as a whole—a structure that will absorb the pre-existing political mechanisms that gave birth to it. (This latter idea is essentially an ultimate evolution of the technostructure model discussed in Chapter 2.) Whichever development path is anticipated—and the two are potentially interactive, not mutually exclusive—in the end, the corporation and the state will have coalesced; nonpolitical avenues for independent rivalry, success, and failure will be foreclosed; and social and political freedom and diversity will be severely curtailed.

The view that increasingly pervasive corporate influence will give rise to increasing demand for government control has been emphasized by Hayek: "The more it comes to be accepted that corporations ought to be directed in the services of specific public interests, the more persuasive becomes the contention that, as government is the appointed guardian of the public interest, government should also have power to tell corporations what they must do."[8] Proponents of this view frequently cite wage- and price-control legislation as evidence of the public's view that business is unable to conduct itself without government intervention. And corporate support of such controls is, to Friedman, striking evidence of the fact that businessmen, "although extremely far-sighted and clear-headed in matters that are internal to their businesses, . . . are incredibly short-sighted and muddle-headed in matters that are outside their businesses but affect the possible survival of business in general. . . . There is nothing that could do more in a brief period to destroy a market system and replace it by a centrally controlled system than effective governmental control of prices and wages."[9]

The alternative scenario is anticipated by Levitt, who terms the result a "New Feudalism." He writes:

> At the rate we are going there is more than a contingent probability that, with all its resounding good intentions, business statesmanship may create the corporate equivalent of the unitary state. Its proliferating employee welfare programs, its serpentine involvement in community, government, charitable and educational affairs, its prodigious currying of political and public favor through hundreds of peripheral preoccupations, all these well-intended but insidious contrivances are greasing the rails for our collective descent into a social order that would be as repugnant to the corporations themselves as to their critics. The danger is that all these things will turn the corporation into a twentieth-century equivalent of the medieval Church. The corporation would eventually invest itself with all-embracing duties, obligations, and finally powers—ministering to the whole man and molding him and society in the image of corporation's narrow ambitions and its essentially unsocial needs.[10]

Levitt's general perspective is substantially the same as that of Friedman and Hayek:

> Welfare and society are not the corporation's business. Its business is making money, not sweet music. The same goes for unions. Their business is "bread and butter" and job rights. In a free enterprise system, welfare is supposed to be automatic; and where it is not, it becomes government's job. This is the concept of pluralism. Government's job is not business and business's job is not government. And unless these functions are resolutely separated in all respects they are eventually combined in every respect. In the end the danger is not that government will run business, or that business will run government,

---

[8] Frederick Hayek, in *Management and Corporations, 1985,* ed. Anshen and Bach, p. 116.

[9] Milton Friedman, *New York Times Magazine,* September 13, 1970.

[10] Theodore Levitt, "The Dangers of Social Responsibility," *Harvard Business Review,* September-October, 1958, p. 41.

but rather than the two of them will coalesce . . . into a single power, unopposed and unopposable.[11]

CRITIQUE OF FUNDAMENTALISM

Since the purpose of this entire book is to present a reasoned alternative to the fundamentalist position—an alternative that also contrasts sharply with the naive and nebulous general concept of "social responsibility"—a detailed critique at this point is neither possible nor desirable. However, the main outlines of such a critique may be briefly indicated, since these points stand on their own, even if our particular alternative view is not adopted.

There are three essential points to be made. They relate to 1) the legal status of business organizations and the "rules of the game"; 2) the validity of the market contract model as a description of social and economic relationships; and 3) the inevitable impact of large, complex, and powerful organizations on the rest of society.

Political and Legal Legitimacy

Even the most ardent fundamentalist would not deny that the business organization must pursue its activities within a constraining framework of legal and social forces. As Friedman points out: "In a free-enterprise, private-enterprise system, a corporate executive is an employee of the owners of the business. He has direct responsibility . . . to conduct the business in accordance with their desire, which generally will be to make as much money as possible while conforming to the basic rules of the society, both those embodied in law and those embodied in ethical custom."[12] Further, since the corporation is specifically a creation of public policy, society has unquestionable authority to issue or retract grants of corporate privilege; and there can be no sense in which social direction or limitation of corporate activity is illegitimate or intrusive. Henry Wallich sums up the situation very succinctly: "In any event, the issue is not whether the private corporation can or cannot legitimately be required by society to perform certain functions. In an age when the corporate income tax rate is 48 percent, it should be obvious that society can make corporations do anything it wants."[13]

The notion of social controls, stimuli, rewards, or penalties is explicitly acknowledged by the fundamentalists in their respect for the "rules of the game." They neglect, however, to consider the fact that the rules are, and must be, constantly changing in response to the needs of society. Hence, they

[11] *Ibid.*, p. 47.

[12] Milton Friedman, *New York Times Magazine,* September 13, 1970.

[13] Henry C. Wallich, "Second Lecture," in *The Modern Corporation and Social Responsibility* ed. Manne and Wallich, p. 39.

fall into the error of arguing that literal adherence to existing rules—which will inevitably diverge somewhat from current needs and behavior patterns—will suffice to ensure satisfactory corporate performance. On the contrary, one might as easily anticipate that rigid adherence to outdated standards might be more likely to cause society to reject the concept of corporate authority altogether and to attempt to invent other and more responsive mechanisms for accomplishing social tasks.

On a broader level, the fundamentalist argument that the legal status of business organizations somehow limits their ability to perform social functions ignores the fact, emphasized in Chapter 2, that formal, legal arrangements tend to confirm and formalize existing relationships, rather than to bring them into being in the first place. Many of the principles of Anglo-American commercial law simply reflect formal recognition of pre-existing customs and traditions. In short, the legal status of the managerial unit is not its principal or determining characteristic. As economic and organizational relationships change over time, the legal and governmental framework of social activity changes as well. Hence, the fundamentalist argument that socially useful tasks cannot be performed by business organizations because of implicit or explicit legal limitations on their activities involves a basic confusion between cause and effect. Over the long run, the political legitimacy of business organizations depends upon their ability to serve the needs of society, not the other way around.

Validity of Market Contract Model

The second main criticism of fundamentalism involves the descriptive validity of the market contract model on which it is based. The point can be simply stated: *The modern economic system does not work that way.* If it were true that all players in the economic game began each round of play with an appropriate stock of resources and abilities so that they could effectively make their preferences known and their skills available through the working of the system, and *if* the system itself worked with acceptable speed and efficiency, it *might* follow that the market contract model would work to produce the economic results anticipated. Actual circumstances depart considerably, however, from these conditions.

Resources and abilities are, in fact, very unevenly distributed among individuals and groups within society, and this initial distribution has a powerful effect on one's ability to participate in the socio-economic game. Further, the game operates on calendar time, and whole lifetimes pass while the "inevitable" forces of the market system are working themselves out. Finally, the combination of initial inequality with operating friction and delay produces numerous situations in which inequities and barriers to participation become greater rather than smaller, excessive rewards and penalties accumulate rather than dissipate, and overall system performance departs more and more substantially from—rather than tending toward—the social optimum. If these conditions describe, even in part, the actual economic and social environment, the market contract model must be regarded as incomplete and inaccurate, and the fundamentalist position based upon it as correspondingly defective.

The reality of large managerial organizations powerful enough to ignore or subvert the pressure of the market contract model can scarcely be questioned. Although competitive pressures and market resistance may eventually turn even the most powerful enterprise away from a socially undesired—and therefore fundamentally "inefficient"—path, the large and well-established corporation possesses great powers of resistance and is governed by pervasive inertia. Thus, it can scarcely be argued that large and powerful firms are subject to the discipline of the market with either the intensity or the speed necessary for effective operation of the market contract mechanism.

Of perhaps even greater importance is the fact that all participants in modern industrial societies do not have equal access to the market mechanism itself. Social preferences are reflected through the market only when the members of society are, in fact, market participants. If persons or groups wishing to offer or obtain goods and services are excluded from the market either by institutional barriers or by simple lack of money, the alternatives and preferences represented by these members of society are not reflected through the market mechanism. Under these circumstances the overall performance of the market economy can be accepted as a social optimum only if the intentions and preferences of the excluded and under-represented members of society are considered irrelevant. Arbitrary exclusion of members of society from the social decision-making process, of course, undermines the philosophical basis for pluralistic democracy itself.

A final issue with respect to the market contract model involves the importance in modern industrial society of goods and services that require collective production and use, and that therefore cannot be efficiently provided and exchanged through individual market transactions. Three types of examples are important: (1) economic activity traditionally associated with the "public utility" concept, such as energy and transportation; (2) environmental qualities, such as clean air and water, noise control, and waste disposal; and (3) social amenities, such as equality of opportunity, the absence of arbitrary discrimination, and special assistance to the disadvantaged. Although these broad types of collective goods are dissimilar in many respects, they share the common attribute that social decisions as to their quantity and cost can rarely be made and implemented through the market contract mechanism. Hence, insofar as collective goods of these several types take on increased importance in the mature industrial societies, the fundamentalist notion that a social optimum can be achieved within the market contract model will prove increasingly unsatisfactory.

Impact of Large Organizations

The third element in the critique of fundamentalism is that the impact of large managerial organizations on the rest of society is obvious and inevitable. Hence, a denial of this impact and a disregard of its implications is neither intellectually nor politically permissible.

Even in their routine market transactions, large corporations affect life styles and aspirations, the physical environment, government, and many other aspects of social life. In addition, these organizations engage in large-scale activities specifically designed to influence their markets and to increase demand for their products. Hence, the notion that these organizations operate simply to fulfill autonomous or "given" social needs as reflected in the market mechanism is preposterous. Institutions shape cultural values, and private economic institutions specifically attempt to shape cultural values in their own interests. This statement implies neither praise nor blame; it is simply a fact. Disregard of these relationships, however, or denial of their existence would indeed be cause for blame.

Finally, there is the issue of power. Large corporations have considerable influence in our society. Their size alone gives rise to it, and their regular operations utilize and increase it. Therefore, they cannot avoid the responsibility that accompanies power in any social setting nor can they reject exercise of power on the basis of incompetence. Few will challenge the fundamentalist argument that successful business managers are not necessarily well-equipped to identify or promote the "public interest." However, these same managers may not be skilled at accounting, marketing, or engineering—required activities for the comduct of business affairs. Their response to the need for more broadly responsible decision making should be the same as their response to the need for any other function within the organization—i.e., develop competence to do the job. An organization's neglect of its societal impact on the basis of admitted incompetence is no more tolerable than neglect of accounting or inventory control on the same grounds. When these functions are part of the organization's basic task, the organization either develops the ability to handle them or goes out of business.

SUMMARY

The fundamentalist position is that the scope of managerial responsibility should be restricted to those functions necessary for the successful accomplishment of its primary tasks, including the market transactions associated with them. Market evaluation is the sole criterion of success; profit opportunity is the sole stimulus for activity.

The case for fundamentalism rests on its alleged consistency with and support of existing economic and political relationships and on the negative appraisal of proposed alternatives. The validity of individual purchase preferences and the effectiveness of market stimuli are basic principles of traditional economic analysis. And the concepts of private property and freedom of contract are deeply engrained in Western legal tradition. Hence, both economic and political theory tend to validate the market contract model and the fundamentalist viewpoint derived from it. Within this context, any diversion of managerial attention to broader social concerns results in both a loss of economic efficiency and in a violation of basic legal restrictions and responsibilities. In the end, departures from the fundamentalist norm will undermine the social and political fabric of society itself.

The critique of fundamentalism is based upon its overemphasis on issues of legal and political legitimacy, on the descriptive invalidity of the market contract model, and on the unquestionable power and impact of large corporations in our society. This critique is continued in the presentation of a variety of "social involvement" views in Chapter 4.

CHAPTER FOUR

The Scope of
Managerial Responsibility:
Socialization and Involvement

The Socialization Process
> The Psychological Setting
> Stages in the Process

Responses to Socialization
> Corporate Philanthropy
> Stylistic and Process Responses
> Citizenship and Coalitions

Critique of "Social Responsibility"

Summary

The rhetoric of American political and social life has clearly been dominated by fundamentalist themes, reflecting an underlying acceptance of the market contract model of management-society relationships. At the same time, the challenge of the exploitation analysis and the emergence of professional management gradually undermined the intellectual and political bases of pure laissez faire liberalism. As a result, there has been a continuing search for an alternative conception of the social role of managerial organizations, a conception that would combine significant reliance on the market mechanism with an acknowledgment of the firm's substantial involvement in society beyond the limited boundaries of market exchange. This search has produced a variety of specific responses, most of them associated with an undefined concept of "social responsibility." Both the search and the responses reflect a gradual process of socialization that has taken place throughout our society and particularly within its large business enterprises, over the past several decades. We therefore consider this socialization process itself before turning to a survey and critique of various "social responsibility" responses.

THE SOCIALIZATION PROCESS

Gradual recognition of an explicit relationship between business management and its social environment, other than that implied by strict fundamentalism, can be appropriately described as the result of a socialization process; that is, a process by which individuals or groups become adapted to a social environment. The process itself is evolutionary. Changes do not occur all at once, nor do they remain fixed after they have occurred. The evolving patterns of attitude and behavior reflect pragmatic reactions to changing circumstances rather than application of a coherent and unified theory. Solutions that "succeed" tend to replace those that "fail," regardless of principle or ideology. Criteria of "success" and "failure," of course, include reducing tension, increasing stability, or in some fashion promoting the welfare of the individuals and groups involved, as well as the economic or market success or failure of individual enterprises.

In spite of the historical prominence of fundamentalist ideology in American society, the actual practice of management has traditionally deviated rather significantly from fundamentalist norms. Economic objectives have not always been pursued with unlimited diligence, nor have noneconomic objectives ever been totally absent from the purview of management. Private business owners and executives have been among the dominant social and political leaders of our society since the earliest times; and—although this leadership role is subject to various interpretations—Letwin observes, "the attitudes of businessmen . . . corresponded pretty well, at most times, to the attitude of most Americans of all classes, occupations, and political outlooks. . . . No fundamental cleavage of outlook between businessmen and the rest ever became a hard-set presumption of American life."[1] In short, the sharp distinction between the viewpoint and interest of the managerial elite and the rest of society—a distinction explicit in both the market contract and exploitation models—has always been more apparent than real.

The Psychological Setting

Some modification of the strict fundamentalist position seems inevitable at the purely personal level under almost any circumstances. The individual manager develops his personal ideology and attitude over time on the basis of all his social contacts and relationships—job, home, community, school, and church. Some of these relationships give rise to compatible and mutually reinforcing conceptions of the manager and his role. Others give rise to conflict and strain. The interplay of these forces produces the individual's own unique ideological perspective. "Businessmen adhere to their particular kind of ideology because of the emotional conflicts, the anxieties, and the doubts

[1] William Letwin, "The Past and Future of the American Businessman," *Daedalus* (American Academy of Arts and Sciences, Proceedings, Winter 1969), XCVIII, No. 1, pp. 14-15.

engendered by the actions which their roles as businessmen compel them to take, and by the conflicting demands of other social roles which they must play in family and community. . . . For the individual businessman, the function of the ideology is to help him maintain his psychological ability to meet the demands of his occupation."[2]

In his position as surrogate for the primeval entrepreneur, the manager may feel constrained to speak of the virtues of capitalism, free markets, and the competitive spirit. In his role as technocrat and citizen, he may simultaneously engage in a variety of contradictory actions, such as philanthropic endeavors, the pursuit of government subsidies, and cooperation with civic projects.

Many pressures in the social environment combine to affect the manager in his decision-making capacity. Bowen's original study concluded that the concern of businessmen about "social responsibility" stemmed from three sources: (1) they were forced to be concerned; (2) they had been persuaded to be more concerned; and (3) conditions had become more amenable to the development and implementation of such concern. As changes arise from all three sources, concern for responsibilities to the public becomes a part of the manager's value set or ideology and, inevitably, enters into the decisions he makes. Such concern becomes, in fact, an additional factor constraining the pursuit of organizational goals, or perhaps even a part of the goals themselves. Bowen observes that, "in general, business is sensitive to changes in the market for its goods and it is equally sensitive to changes in the market for the business system itself. In both markets, it will rise to what is expected of it—but it will not rise much higher than that and if public opinion relaxes and expects less of business, some of the gains of the century could easily be lost."[3]

Stages in the Process

The fundamentalist view defines business responsibility primarily in terms of activities, with the ultimate criterion of success being the willingness of other members of society to reward the firm through the market exchange mechanism for the performance of its specific functions. By contrast, alternative views of the scope of managerial responsibility involve the recognition of many sources and forms of social approval and disapproval. An organization's impact upon its "many relevant publics" then becomes the basis for identifying and appraising its role in society as a whole. The process by which the latter view comes to replace the former involves three stages: recognition, consideration, and positive reaction.

---

[2] Francis X. Sutton, Seymour E. Harris, Carl Kaysen, and James Tobin, *The American Business Creed* (Cambridge, Mass.: Harvard University Press, 1956), p. 11.

[3] Howard R. Bowen, *Social Responsibilities of the Businessman* (New York: Harper & Brothers, 1953), p. 106.

A "public," as that term is used here, is a group of persons bound together by a common interest. "Publics" are not mutually exclusive, and an individual may be a member of several different publics simultaneously. A public becomes "relevant" to an organization whenever its unifying interest is one that affects, or is affected by, the organization's own activities. Recognition of the existence of relevant publics can occur in several ways. The organization may seek to develop and maintain contact with such publics on its own initiative, as with groups of potential customers, suppliers, and so on. Or, a relevant public may be defined by legal requirements, as in the case of collective-bargaining agents or local governments. Or, members of the public themselves may use direct pressure to bring their existence and viewpoint to the attention of organizational managers. In any event, the first stage in the socialization process involves the recognition that such publics exist and that the sphere of managerial impact is not limited to the particular social groups with which (or the purposes *for* which) it engages in market exchange.

The second stage in the socialization process goes beyond mere recognition to an acknowledgment that management has some responsibility to consider its impact upon such publics in the process of making decisions and conducting its activities.[4] Such impact may, of course, be clearly "positive," and its consideration may simply reinforce and confirm the wisdom of managerial decisions already taken. The core of the socialization process is reached, however, when "negative" impacts are identified and their consequences explicitly introduced into managerial decision making. Negative impacts may be essentially economic—such as the reduction of operating efficiency in a product, an increase in accident hazards, or loss of employment opportunities—or they may be essentially social or ethical in character. In either case, the consideration of negative social impact—and the implication that decisions might be modified to reduce such impact—is now generally recognized as an essential element in the managerial process.

The second stage of socialization is forcefully affirmed in one of the leading business policy texts:

> We come at last to the . . . final component of strategy—the moral aspects of choice. In our consideration of strategic alternatives, we have so far moved from what the strategist *might* and *can* do to what he *wants* to do; we now move to what he *ought* to do—from the point of view of society and his own inner standards of right and wrong. Ethics, like preference, may be considered a question of value. To some the suggestion that an orderly and analytical process of strategy determination must find its way through the tangle of ethics is repugnant. . . . While fully aware of the problems involved, we contend that the businessman must examine the impact on the public good of the policy alternatives he is free to elect and implement.[5]

[4] Kenneth R. Andrews, "Public Responsibility in the Private Corporation," *The Journal of Industrial Economics,* XX, No. 2 (1972), 135ff.

[5] Edmund P. Learned, C. Roland Christensen, Kenneth R. Andrews, and William D. Guth, *Business Policy: Text and Cases* (Homewood, Illinois: Richard D. Irwin, Inc., 1969), p. 578.

Although the first and second stages of the socialization process that we have described here tend to merge—recognition of relevant publics occurring simultaneously with consideration of their specific viewpoints or demands —the third stage stands clearly apart. In the third stage, the organization develops a positive stance of its own with respect to some or all of the many publics. The desires and goals of the several publics are no longer viewed as "constraints" on otherwise desirable decisions or patterns of behavior. By contrast, the goals of the "publics" become incorporated into the goals of the organization itself, serving to define its overall objectives and norms. Adoption of such positive stance involves, in essence, an organizational decision to become further socialized, to interact with the relevant publics in the identification of common purposes and the solution of common problems. The third stage also brings into sharp prominence the need to delineate a boundary for managerial responsibility encompassing something less than the full range of activities and concerns of society itself.

RESPONSES TO SOCIALIZATION

As the socialization process proceeds, organizational management begins to alter its behavior—or, at least, its rhetoric—in response to a new sense of involvement in society. The response may lead to changes in both the *process* of management and the *substance* of managerial decisions. In fact, changes in both process and substance usually occur at the same time; and since the socialization process itself is evolutionary and irregular among organizations and situations, the range of responses actually encountered is also extremely diverse. Within this great variety of behavior and experience, a few major themes and clusters of activity stand out, which we have grouped under three major headings: Corporate Philanthropy; Stylistic and Process Responses; and Citizenship and Coalitions, often termed the "profit plus" philosophy.

Corporate Philanthropy

At the first stage of the socialization process described above, when business managers have become aware that their organizations exist within a larger society and that this larger society may have needs or goals that are not completely achieved through market exchange, the obvious response is philanthropy—gifts by the corporation to specific individuals or institutions on the basis of perceived need or general social value. [6]

---

[6] Major references on corporate philanthropy include: Richard Eells, *Corporate Giving in a Free Society* (New York: Harper & Brothers, 1956); Richard Eells, *The Corporation and the Arts* (New York: The Macmillan Company, 1967); Marion R. Fremont-Smith, *Philanthropy and the Business Corporation* (New York: Russell Sage Foundation, 1972); Alvin H. Reiss, *Culture and Company* (New York: Twayne Publishing Company, 1972); Morrel Heald, *The Social Responsibilities of Business: Company and Community, 1900-1960* (Cleveland: The Press

Corporate philanthropy has been a significant source of charitable funding for many years. It has been estimated that in 1970 approximately one billion dollars was donated to health and welfare, education, the arts, civic, and other causes by American companies.[7] Since the extent of an individual company's giving reflects its resources, the demands made upon it for assistance, and the attitude of its management, there are wide variations in philanthropic behavior among companies. In 1970, the average rate of company contributions among companies surveyed by the Conference Board amounted to .82% of pre-tax corporate income; another source reports corporate philanthropy amounting to about 1% of net profit.[8]

The modern form of corporate philanthropy derives directly from the strong ethical and religious concerns of some of the "robber barons," men who accumulated fortunes—not always through morally acceptable means—during the rapid industrialization of the late nineteenth century. The leader and archetype figure of this movement was Andrew Carnegie, who declared it the "duty of the man of wealth . . . to consider all surplus revenues . . . as trust funds, which he is called upon to administer . . . in the manner which, in his judgment, is best calculated to produce the most beneficial results for the community. . . ." He is thus "the mere trustee and agent for his poorer brethren, bringing to their service his superior wisdom, experience and ability to administer, doing for them better than they would or could do for themselves."[9]

From its scattered and highly individualistic beginnings, the idea of corporate philanthropy became accepted over the following decades as a routine managerial activity, institutionalized particularly in the community chest movement. However, two legal problems arose. One was the fact that such gifts were not deductible for tax purposes. This obstacle was removed in 1935, when Congress authorized the deduction of charitable contributions up to 5% of pre-tax profits in the computation of federal income taxes on corporations. (Personal tax deductions for contributions dated back to 1917.)

The second and more complex issue was the legitimacy of management's distribution of corporate earnings for charitable purposes without receiving any specific organizational benefits in return. The legality of such distribu-

---

of Case Western Reserve University, 1970); and Frank G. Dickinson, *The Changing Position of Philanthropy in the American Economy* (New York: National Bureau of Economic Research, Inc., 1970).

[7] John H. Watson, III, *Biennial Survey of Company Contributions* (New York: The Conference Board, 1972).

[8] *Ibid.*, and also William J. Baumol, "Enlightened Self-Interest and Corporate Philanthropy," in *A New Rationale for Corporate Social Policy* (Lexington, Mass.: D.C. Heath & Company, 1970), pp. 3-19.

[9] Andrew Carnegie, *The Gospel of Wealth*, ed. Edward C. Kirkland (Cambridge: Harvard University Press, 1962), p. 25. (Quoted in Heald, *Social Responsibilities*, p. 17.)

tions was finally resolved in a landmark case, in which the court reasoned as follows:

> When the wealth of the nation was primarily in the hands of individuals they discharged their responsibilities as citizens by donating freely for charitable purposes. With the transfer of most of the wealth to corporate hands and the imposition of heavy burdens of individual taxation, they have been unable to keep pace with increased philanthropic needs. They have therefore, with justification, turned to corporations to assume the modern obligations of good citizenship in the same manner as humans do. . . . It seems to us as the conditions prevailing when corporations were originally created required that they serve public as well as private interests, modern conditions require that corporations acknowledge and discharge social as well as private responsibilities as members of the communities within which they operate. Within this broad concept there is no difficulty in sustaining, as incidental to their proper objects and in aid of the public welfare, the power of corporations to contribute corporate funds within reasonable limits . . . [the contribution in question] was voluntarily made in the reasonable belief that it would aid the public welfare and advance the interests of the plaintiff as a private corporation and as part of the community in which it operates.[10]

Several features of corporate philanthropy, as a response to the recognition of social involvement, should be noted. In general, philanthropic activity is only remotely related (if related at all) to the corporation's specialized role or primary operations; neither is it typically aimed at "relevant publics" in the usual sense. On the contrary, philanthropy may be aimed at general community goodwill—as in the case of United Fund activities—or at special objects of managerial favor, such as universities, hospitals, and local or national charities. Increasingly, both large and middle-sized corporations have established separate corporate foundations, usually with boards and administrative officers somewhat overlapping with those of the firm itself, for the purpose of philanthropic activity. Yet even in these instances, the foundations generally serve as conduits for funds to other institutions operating in spheres unrelated to that of the donor. Corporate contributors, unlike individuals contributing from their personal wealth or family holdings, rarely involve themselves directly in the activities or policies of the agencies that their funds ultimately support.

Stylistic and Process Responses

At the second stage of the socialization process, when a managerial organization decides to include its impact on a particular "public" as a consideration in its decision making, some change generally occurs in the *way* things are done—i.e., in the managerial *process*. Examples of process changes are the establishment of committees composed of diverse representatives from

[10] *A.P. Smith Mfg. Co.* v. *Barlow*, 13 N.J. 145, 98 A.2d 581 (1953).

within the organization, formal solicitation of the views of employees and customers, installation of consumer "hot lines," appointment of "outside" directors, and other overt evidences of an attempt to introduce new perspectives into the process of management. In practice, of course, it is entirely possible that ethical or stylistic considerations may be introduced into managerial decision making without any corresponding formal or structural change occurring. And it is also possible that the formal change may be the *only* change—i.e., that only the *style* but not the *substance* of managerial activity will be altered. However, since style is itself an aspect of social interaction, a change in style alone may represent a significant response to socialization.

Much of the recent discussion of corporate "social responsibility" appears to place primary emphasis on stylistic or process responses. Such responses—desirable through they may be—typically involve no specific consideration of the cost of "social responsibility" and no explicit change in the goals of the organization. Emphasis is placed on the *way* the organization conducts its affairs. And even if changes in the managerial process do result in changes in the substantive results as well, no formal attempt is made to discover just what change has occurred or with what ultimate effect. Some examples of style and process responses are discussed in more detail in Chapter 8.

Citizenship and Coalitions

The term *corporate citizenship* suggests some expansion of organizational goals to include a specific commitment to responsibilities in the larger social environment and reflects the beginning of the final stage of the socialization process. The added responsibilities may be specifically limited to the local community—e.g., neighborhood and environmental effects, development of business opportunities, transportation facilities, or educational institutions, and so forth—or may involve the recognition of a citizenship role in society at large.

Corporate citizenship involves at least two distinct elements not necessarily involved in either philanthropy or in the stylistic-process response to socialization. The first of these elements is explicit acceptance of organizational *goals* beyond the scope of market exchange transactions; the second is recognition of the need for *coalitions* among interested parties for the purpose of accomplishing mutually desired goals.

The addition of citizenship goals to the usual organizational objectives may be termed the "profit-plus" philosophy. The essential idea is that the survival-growth-profitability goals of the firm are expanded to include a citizenship element as well. The new element does not supplant the old, nor are both fully integrated into a new comprehensive framework. Nevertheless, there may well be some sacrifice of short-run advantage, including profit, in order to attain the "plus," the social objective that has been explicitly included among the goals of the firm. As the Committee for Economic Development (CED) put it:

> It is in the "enlightened self-interest" of corporations to promote the public welfare in a positive way. The doctrine has gradually been developing in business and public policy over the past several decades to the point where it supports widespread corporate practices of a social nature, ranging from philanthropy to investments in attractive plants and other programs designed to improve the company's social environment. . . . Since major corporations have especially long planning horizons, they may be able to incur costs and forego profits in the short run for social improvements that are expected to enhance profits or improve the corporate environment in the long run.[11]

The specific activities that may be included in a "profit-plus" approach are many and varied. All types of involvement in the physical and managerial aspects of local community life are included. So are policies like encouraging employee participation in community affairs, lending executives to government or public service activities, establishing urban affairs departments, and sponsoring specific service activities, such as health and recreation programs, for members of the community at large. The reasons for undertaking particular activities, the limits to be set for them, and the purpose and guidelines to be pursued often remain obscure.

The citizenship approach usually involves individual firms in a search for coalitions—groups of organizations and interests, united by a common problem and a willingness to pool efforts in developing a solution.[12] In some instances, a natural coalition arises to deal with a problem that has multiple sources or impacts. One firm that discharges effluent into a lake is likely to be unable to solve the resulting pollution problem by restricting or even eliminating its own discharges; but in concert with all other entities discharging into the lake, a solution may be possible.

Since coalitions are voluntary associations, their existence and vitality are entirely dependent upon the commitment of the members to the group. They are not self-generating, and experience has shown that they can be quite fragile. The need for a coalition approach must be perceived by at least one organization or participant, and others must be persuaded of the value and importance of the common goal. Once organized, coalitions serve to expand the range of methods an organization may use in dealing with social problems beyond the control of its immediate management. However, maintenance of a successful working coalition is highly dependent upon a common view among the members as to the scope of their responsibilities and their range of alternatives. Some examples of coalition activity are discussed in Chapters 8 and 9.

[11] Committee for Economic Development (CED), *Social Responsibilities of Business Corporations* (New York: CED, 1971), pp. 27-33.

[12] John McDonald, "How Social Responsibility Fits the Game of Business," *Fortune,* December, 1970, p. 104.

CRITIQUE OF "SOCIAL RESPONSIBILITY"

Commendable and well-intentioned as many responses to the gradual process of corporate socialization may have been, the general doctrine of corporate "social responsibility" has been fairly described as an "elusive concept . . . about which so much froth has been written."[13] Even among its strongest supporters, the doctrine itself remains vague and ill-defined. Thus it provides no basis for dealing concretely with possible conflicts between traditional corporate goals and social objectives; and it suggests no boundary between the genuine responsibilities of business management and the entire range of activity within the host society. The CED statement explicitly affirms this unlimited purview: "Indeed, the corporate interest broadly defined by management can support involvement in helping to solve *virtually any social problem . . .* [Italics added]."[14]

But the more seriously one takes the basic fact of corporate social involvement, the more dissatisfied one becomes with such nonoperational guidelines. It is evidently not possible for individual corporations, even very large ones, to take an active role in every sphere of economic and social life. Indeed, a "do whatever you can" principle is essentially unworkable because it provides no real guidance for identifying specific goals and assigning priorities. And, being unworkable, "do whatever you can" becomes a justification for doing nothing at all, or—at best—for uneven and unrelated endeavors, based on transient and personal enthusiasms, or *ad hoc* pressures, rather than long-term organizational plans and commitments.

The concept of "enlightened self-interest" occupies a conspicuous and troublesome place in the social responsibility literature. As the CED statement puts it: "Enlightened self-interest . . . has both "carrot and stick" aspects. There is the positive appeal to the corporation's greater opportunities to grow and profit in a healthy, prosperous, and well-functioning society. And there is the negative threat of increasingly onerous compulsion and harassment if it does not do its part in helping create such a society." [15]

The emphasis on self-interest can give rise to an impression, perhaps entirely unjustified, that the whole affair is merely a subterfuge, an extension of the advertising and public relations function. Indeed, Manne insists that the self-interest argument implies that the corporation is simply discovering new and necessary dimensions of its basic job and still evaluating each decision against the fundamentalist test of profitability.[16] If Manne's posi-

[13] Neil W. Chamberlain, *The Limits of Corporate Responsibility* (New York: Basic Books, Inc., 1973), p. 204.

[14] CED, *Social Responsibilities of Business Corporations*, p. 27.

[15] *Ibid.*, p. 29.

[16] Henry G. Manne, "First Lecture," in *The Modern Corporation and Social Responsibility*, Henry G. Manne and Henry C. Wallich (Washington, D.C.: American Enterprise Institute for Public Policy Research, 1972).

tion is correct, it would appear that the doctrine of self-interest—like the individual owner or manager's concept of philanthropy—could justify any act not clearly destructive of the fabric of society. At best, the self-interest theme suggests a policy of making separate and minimal responses to the most critical threats and pressures, not a fundamentally altered perspective on the relationship between the business firm and its host environment.

The most telling criticism of the "social responsibility" doctrine is its fundamental lack of substance. It fails to provide any clear guidance for selecting appropriate areas of activity or for establishing goals and appraisal criteria within any particular area. As Friedman argues, even if the corporate executive can get away with spending other people's money for social purposes, "How is he to know how to spend it? . . . How is he to know what action of his will contribute to [any particular] end? . . . Even if he could answer these questions, how much cost is justified . . .? What is his appropriate share and what is the appropriate share for others?"[17] To put the matter concretely, if a corporation were to offer a bonus for the division or manager achieving the highest level of social performance—in addition to the usual bonuses for profit contribution or sales growth—how will anyone decide who should get it, and how could that decision be explained to the rest of the organization?

In short, all of the varied responses to a vague sense of "social responsibility" reveal a fatal flaw—an absence of boundaries to the scope of managerial responsibility and an absence of criteria for appraising managerial performance, either with respect to the specified areas selected for concern or the decisions and actions taken. Any phase of social life can become the focus of corporate philanthropy. And there is no limit to the search for, or demands of, "relevant publics"; no way to decide when changes in management style and processes have gone too far (or even in the wrong direction); no clear distinction between citizenship and constructive coalitions on one hand and interference and conspiracy on the other.

Overall, these "social responsibility" views and responses are merely way stations on any evolutionary path that must lead to a redefinition of the social role of the managerial organization itself, a redefinition reflecting both the impact of the socialization process that has taken place and the inescapable need for boundaries and guidelines for genuine responsibility, accountability, and evaluation. In Chapter 7, we attempt to offer such a redefinition, described as the *principle of public responsibility,* based upon the interpenetrating systems model of management-society relations presented in Chapter 2, the critiques of both fundamentalism and vague "social responsibility" viewpoints presented in this and the preceding chapter, and the analysis of the public policy process set forth in Chapters 5 and 6.

[17] Milton Friedman, "The Social Responsibility of Business Is to Increase Its Profits," *New York Times Magazine,* September 13, 1970.

SUMMARY

As a result of a gradual process of socialization, the notion is now very widely accepted that private business organizations are, in some general sense, involved in the larger society and have some responsibility to take into account their general social impact. The sequential stages of the process are typically associated with different types of responses. Initial recognition of social involvement is particularly associated with corporate philanthropy and with a passive citizenship role. The corporation responds to requests for aid or cooperation but avoids taking initiative or developing a positive stance of its own. Stylistic and process responses are particularly associated with the second stage of socialization, in which an attempt is made to bring previously neglected considerations or viewpoints into the managerial process on a regular basis. Finally, the third stage of socialization—development of a positive stance—implies a conscious attempt to identify appropriate areas of managerial concern and to formulate positive proposals about them.

Each of these responses may be praiseworthy in itself. However, neither the individual responses nor the vague principles that underlie them provide adequate guidance for regular managerial activity or adequate standards for evaluating performance. The criticisms of naive "social responsibility" doctrines as involving mere self-interest on the one hand, or as simply reflecting personal tastes and *ad hoc* pressures on the other, are not entirely unjustified.

Our own view—embodied in *the principle of public responsibility*—is intended to correct these deficiencies. However, this principle cannot be fully presented without reference to the nature of public policy and the policy-formation process, which are the subjects of the next two chapters.

CHAPTER FIVE

The Public Policy Process

Public policy—the process of social decision-making and the substance of the decisions made—is the focus of attention in this and the following chapter for two reasons. First, it is an essential aspect of the social environment within which micro-managerial units operate and is therefore of substantive significance regardless of one's particular view of the management-society relationship. Second, the principle of public responsibility, which embodies our own view of this relationship, explicitly states that public policy is—along with the market mechanism—the source of guidelines and criteria for managerial behavior. Clearly, the implications of this proposition cannot be fully explored without a prior exposition of the nature of public policy and the policy-making process.

THE NATURE OF PUBLIC POLICY

The term *policy* was defined in Chapter 1 as "principles guiding action." The line between basic *policy* and less comprehensive tactical or programmatic decisions, or even routine actions, may, in practice, be difficult to draw. However, as Bauer remarks, "For those [decisions] which have the widest ramifications and the longest time perspective, and which generally require the most information and contemplation, we tend to reserve the term policy."[1]

Public policy refers to widely shared and generally acknowledged principles directing and controlling actions that have broad implications for society at large or major portions thereof. It is not necessary, of course, that all members of society accept, or even be aware of, policy principles and their implications. Even in democratic societies, basic public policies rarely arise from the expression of formal preferences by a majority of the electorate. Indeed, broad segments of society may be specifically excluded from the policy-making process, and particular policies may be designed to oppress or hinder individual social groups. However, whatever the policy-making process in a particular society, the issues dealt with in that process constitute the public policy *agenda,* and the resulting goals and guidelines constitute the substance of public *policy* itself.

Although this definition of public policy is rather sweeping, more limited conceptions—such as Dye's definition: "Public policy is whatever governments choose to do or not to do"[2] —seem to us inadequate. For one thing, some of the most fundamental and far-reaching principles of public policy are only implicit, not explicit, in the actions of government. Yet, inaction (which we take to be the implication of ". . . or not to do") may reflect omission or oversight rather than the affirmation of policy. Further, in our society there are many different levels and organs of "government," and each of them may "do" things as mild and inconsequential as passing resolutions or issuing press releases on one hand, or as substantial as executing criminals, compelling military service, confiscating property, and collecting taxes on the other. Many of these acts constitute, or at least reflect, important aspects of public policy; others have no such broad implications and may even contravene explicit and fundamental policy principles.

These points are worthy of more extended discussion. Anthropologists often emphasize that the critical differentiating features of societies are not their physical or formal characteristics but the ideas that are taken for granted. Hence, the most fundamental principles of public policy may be those that are implicit rather than explicit, viewpoints and goals so widely

---

[1] Raymond A. Bauer and Kenneth J. Gergen, eds., *The Study of Policy Formation* (New York: The Free Press, 1971), p. 2.

[2] Thomas R. Dye, *Understanding Public Policy* (Englewood Cliffs, N.J.: Prentice-Hall, Inc., 1972), p. 1.

shared by the members of society that a need to question them or write them down has never arisen. It is, for example, taken for granted in our society that most property, and particularly the resources and facilities used in the production of goods and services, will be held by private owners; that the selection of products to be produced, production methods, operating locations, and prices will be left to the discretion of micro-unit managers; and that the price mechanism will be primarily relied upon to allocate the resulting output among possible users and, hence, to direct the pattern of economic activity over the long run.

These are sweeping and fundamental principles of social organization, and they underlie many of the actions (and inactions) of government with respect to economic activity. Yet it is notable that they are nowhere explicitly written down and affirmed by any important organ of government as the basis for economic life in our society. On the contrary, they are reflected in official documents principally by indirection, as in detailed enactments that implicitly incorporate these broad principles. The general principles are, paradoxically, most clearly affirmed by the adoption of specific exceptions to them. The host of relevant exceptions includes expansion of public production of goods and services (energy, transportation, health care), prohibitions and requirements concerning product quality, plant location, operating practices, and so forth; and specific controls over production and prices, adopted either as an emergency measure or as a permanent feature of some sector of the economy.

These examples suffice to illustrate the point that fundamental public policy principles may be much broader than, and only implicit in, the legislative enactments of governments. At the same time, it is important to emphasize that formal adoption of a policy statement or passage of legislation alone does not necessarily reveal the substance of public policy. On the contrary, even if purely political rhetoric and deceptive parliamentary tactics are discounted entirely, many explicit and serious legislative enactments, court decisions, and executive orders fail to provide a firm basis for policy development. In the first place, there are problems of interpretation and ambiguity. The apparently unambiguous statement in the Declaration of Independence that "all men are created equal" was followed by almost one hundred years of tolerance of human slavery. And an even longer period elapsed before the federal authority to regulate "commerce," set forth in the Constitution, was interpreted without argument to include manufacturing activities.

Secondly, even when substantive implications are not in debate, intended policies go unrealized because of inadequate financial and political support, incompetent or deliberately inappropriate administration, and the sheer difficulty of implementation even when both resources and intentions are favorable. Indeed, the substantive content of policy depends not only on the adoption, or implicit acceptance, of basic principles, but also on the character and extent of their implementation. In this regard, the emphasis on *action* (and inaction) in Dye's definition—"whatever governments choose to *do* or *not* to do"—is sound.[3]

THE HIERARCHY OF POLICY FORMS

Recognition that the principles of public policy may be found, at one extreme, in the broadly accepted norms and values of society and, at the other extreme, in the detailed conditions of implementation, suggests that there may be a spectrum or hierarchy of forms that public policy may take. Indeed, this is the case. At the risk of considerable oversimplification, we emphasize four key forms in which public policy principles may be articulated: implicit norms and standards, explicit prohibitions and requirements, programs, and indirect guidelines and stimuli.[4]

Implicit Norms and Standards

Enough has been said already to indicate the prevasiveness and importance of implicit but widely shared ideas as basic principles of public policy. It may be useful to emphasize that such implicit principles need not always be benign. On the contrary, widespread acceptance of chauvinistic nationalism or of doctrines of social or racial inferiority, for example, may be viewed as highly undesirable social characteristics. Nevertheless, whatever one's personal evaluation, these and other debatable propositions have been important implicit, as well as explicit, elements of public policy in this and other countries over long periods of time.

Explicit Prohibitions and Requirements

The corpus of formal *law,* implemented by administrative decree and interpreted by courts, is the principal means by which societies reveal their fundamental principles and regulate relationships among their members. Whether conceived as elevated principle ("Not under Man, but under God and Law") or simple fact (According to the story, Judge Roy Bean *was* "The law west of the Pecos"), the notion of law as establishing the essential norms of society is commonplace within developed societies.

The corpus of law regulates both the relationships of members of society among themselves and also the relationships between them, individually and

[3] Our broad conception of the nature of public policy and of its critical importance as a guide to managerial attitudes and behavior is strongly parallel to that presented in John J. Corson, *Business in the Humane Society* (New York: McGraw-Hill Book Company, 1971).

[4] Our general orientation here is strongly influenced by A. D. Lindsay, *The Modern Democratic State* (New York: Oxford University Press, 1943) paperback edition, 1969; and Theodore J. Lowi, *The End of Liberalism* (New York: W. W. Norton & Company, Inc., 1969). See also Dow Votaw, "Traditional Business Concepts Versus Reality: The Role of the State in the Gap Between" in *The Corporate Dilemma* Dow Votaw and S. Prakash Sethi (Englewood Cliffs, N.J.: Prentice-Hall, Inc., 1973).

collectively, and their governmental structure. For example, murder of one member of society by another is not only declared to be a crime, but the authority to determine guilt and mete out punishment is reserved to government itself. Thus, private persons are not only prohibited, in effect, from committing murder they are also prohibited from punishing murderers. (The fact that both crimes and the apprehension-punishment of criminals are sometimes carried out by private parties does not alter the clear and specific content of public policy in this regard. However, if random homicides were generally tolerated or "frontier justice" the rule, then the character of effective public policy would be substantially different.)

One of the virtues of explicit law as a repository of public policy is that obvious inconsistencies or lacunae involving both principles and implementation procedures can be detected. Another is that when controversies arise—what *is* public policy in this area, anyway?—resort can be had to formal authority in search of an answer. (Of course, for both implicit policies and inadvertent omissions, the answer may appear to be "there is none.") Further, the U.S. governmental structure establishes an explicit order of authority—federal law over state law and judicial review of legislative action, for example—such that final arbitration or interpretation may be obtained. It is no small virtue to have a governmental structure within which answers—whatever their content—to specific policy questions can be obtained.

Programs

Programs are the operating activities by which governmental units attempt to discharge the functions assigned to them in the carrying out of public policy. Establishing, financing, directing, and operating a police force, for example, is a central element in a community's local security program. Programs are important in the public policy hierarchy because they determine in very important ways the actual thrust and impact of policy principles. The existence of public programs for carrying out policies does not, of course, necessarily eliminate the role of private organizations in the same policy areas. Although some activities—such as national defense—may be relegated entirely to public control, others may involve combinations of private and public activity, and in still other instances the public program may restrict itself entirely to the guidance, assistance, or stimulation of private endeavors.

Two particular features of programmatic policy, as distinguished from legal requirements and prohibitions, require emphasis. One is that it is relatively easy for conflicts and inconsistencies to develop among programs that are intended to implement the same basic policy principle, or even for programs to work against the very principles they are desired to promote. Such instances of inconsistency or counter-productivity may readily escape detection because the programs themselves are vast and complex, and because procedures and standards of evaluation are absent or insufficient. Significant questions in program evaluation are whether or not the program is operating so as to accomplish its formal objectives, and whether both the legislative basis and program content can be altered to achieve greater congruence with overall policy goals.

A second feature of some importance is that it is possible for programs to be established where no governing policy principle exists. According to Moynihan, the substitution of programs for policy—that is, a confusion between means and ends—was a significant source of conflict and disappointment with respect to social change in the U.S. during the 1960s. As he draws the distinction: "Programs relate to a single part of the [social] system; policy seeks to respond to the system in its entirety." He argues that explicit policy formulation is a necessary prelude to program development and administration, so that questions of program evaluation and effectiveness can then, at least in principle, be answered.[5]

Guidelines and Stimuli

In addition to enacting formal requirements and prohibitions, and in addition to accomplishing tasks through public programs, society at large can direct, encourage, or retard the activities of its members by indicating guidelines and creating stimuli to which they may react. Most such guidelines and stimuli arise through the political or governmental process, although some may originate entirely with private individuals and groups. Widespread public concern with environmental protection problems is proably the most impressive recent example of a public policy issue brought to light and to a significant stage of implementation without the broad participation of governmental agencies. Eventually, of course, when these problems were accorded formal public policy recognition, the full panoply of laws and programs was brought into play.

Guidelines and stimuli can range all the way from general declarations of policy and intent, unsupported by law, budget, or program, to specific criteria and procedures incorporated into extensive programs. It is one thing to affirm the desirability of "equal job opportunities for all Americans" in a political speech and quite another to provide incentive payments or special contract considerations for firms employing previously disadvantaged workers. Guidelines and stimuli can be general or specific, strong or weak, and can be embodied in laws and programs or merely in pronouncements.

The importance of even relatively weak guidelines and informal stimuli, however, is often considerably greater than their immediate impact may suggest. Because these minimal forms of public policy initiative need not require statutory enactment or budgetary status—and because they can arise almost entirely from public opinion itself, rather than from within the political process—they become both harbingers of basic policy change and tests of pos-

[5] Daniel P. Moynihan, "Policy vs. Program in the '70's," *The Public Interest*, No. 20 (Summer 1970), pp. 91, 99.

sible policy formulations and standards. Societal response to initial guidelines and stimuli may also have an important impact on the subsequent path of public policy evolution. For example, if the simple expedient of special tax reduction (or increase) can serve to stimulate private firms to expand (or contract) their activities in a direction desired by public policy, formal direction and enforcement activity—still less establishment of public programs to obtain the desired result—may be unnecessary. This principle was successfully applied to encourage new capital investment through an "investment tax credit" during the 1960s; attempts to apply it to controlling environmental pollution and increasing minority employment have been less ambitious and much less successful.

Each of these forms in which public policy principles may be expressed—and, to repeat, the choice of these four categories alone represents a vast oversimplification—constitutes a means by which society at large attempts to enunciate its own goals and the means it considers appropriate to attain them. Indeed, the means—i.e., the laws and programs—are important parts of the goals themselves. (We may wish to reduce unemployment, but not by executing the unemployed!) Possibilities of conflict within the hierarchy of forms—and, in a large and complex society, among the levels and branches of government and among nongovernment indicators of public opinion—raises many critical questions. Hence, we must turn to a more detailed consideration of the process of public policy formation itself.

MODELS OF THE POLICY PROCESS

Who is the *public* that has the *public policy*? This question must be examined not only in terms of social and political groups and interests but also in terms of the way in which various types of interests and considerations entering into the policy process merge and interact. In an all-powerful dictatorship, public policy could be easily explained as the will or whim of the absolute ruler. In a simple town meeting, policy can be equally well described as the collective judgment of the citizens. But in large and complex societies such as our own, no simple description will suffice to summarize the process of interaction between various groups and individuals, private interests and government bodies, through which public policy is formed. As Bauer emphasizes, "The policy process is a social process and not an intellectual process. Intellectual processes are part of the policy process but ignoring the social processes produces misconceptions of a crucial nature.[6]

Although no simple model describes the whole of the policy process, a number of concepts found in the literature are useful for summarizing certain of its key aspects. In this section three important policy-process ideas—

[6] Raymond A. Bauer, "Social Psychology and the Study of Policy Formation," *American Psychologist*, XXI, No. 10 (1966), pp. 933-42.

optimization, incrementalism, and power-bargaining—are summarized. [7] The final section of the chapter presents a holistic institutional-systems model in which these and other theoretical processes, as well as the institutional structure of government and society, can be integrated. This institutional-systems model is utilized in the remainder of the book as the source of the public policy agenda and of policy guidelines for managerial decision making and performance.

Optimization

Scientists, engineers, most economists, and many bureaucrats tend to regard the public policy process as the rational search for optimal solutions to well-defined problems. The elementary principles are *maximization* (attaining the highest possible level of output or results for a given level of input or effort) and *minimization* (incurring the least possible cost or inconvenience in order to achieve a given result). It is obvious at once that both the character of the desired results—the performance qualities to be maximized—and the nature of the required inputs—the elements to be minimized—must be known or hypothesized before an optimization problem can be formulated. Uncertainty with respect to the precise relationship between inputs and outputs, efforts and rewards, can be formally taken into account by means of probability analysis.

The choice among public policy alternatives can be described as an optimization problem within the familiar context of welfare economics or production theory. Suppose that there are two different public policy goals—for example, a high rate of economic growth and adequate protection for national defense—and suppose further that (a) the total amount of resources that can be devoted to the two goals (which might, in fact, be all the resources of the economy left after provision is made for current consumption) is known; and (b) that the goal-achievement results themselves do not interact in some complex way (e.g., economic growth does not by itself generate or undermine national defense, and vice versa). Then we may depict the possible results of using various amounts of resources to achieve each of the two goals in performance functions like those shown in Figure 5-1 (A) and (B). We assume that all resources can be used to make some contribution to economic growth, so that the performance function, although reflecting decreasing returns, never reaches a true maximum. Its greatest value is attained when all resources are devoted to this goal alone. By contrast, we assume that some resources are of no use whatsoever for national defense, so that maximum national defense can be achieved—although, again, with

---

[7] This brief discussion can scarcely suggest the great variety, depth, and interest of the policy-process literature. Major references, in addition to Dye, *Understanding Public Policy,* and Bauer and Gergen, *The Study of Policy Formation,* include: Yehezkel Dror, *Public Policy-making Reexamined* (Scranton, Pa.: Chandler Publishing Company, 1968); Harold D. Lasswell, *A Preview of Policy Sciences* (New York: Elsevier, 1971); and Charles Lindblom, *The Policy-Making Process* (Englewood Cliffs, N.J.: Prentice-Hall, Inc., 1968).

FIGURE 5-1

Performance Functions

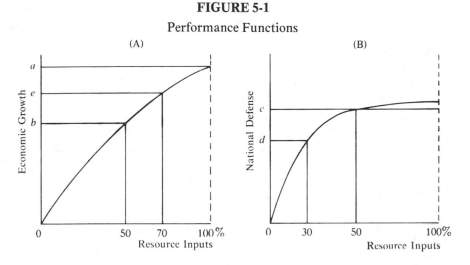

decreasing returns—with only a portion of the total available resources; additional inputs yield no performance results whatsoever.

In Figure 5-2 the information contained in Figure 5-1 (A) and (B) is combined to show the trade-off relationships between economic growth and national defense, as alternative uses of resources. If all available resources are devoted to economic growth, a performance level of *a* for growth can be attained, along with zero national defense. By contrast, if only half of all available resources are devoted to defense—with the remaining half devoted to economic growth—then a level of *c* (the maximum) national defense can be obtained along with a level *b* of growth. Between the combinations (*a* growth and zero defense) and (*b* growth and *c* defense) there is a regular

FIGURE 5-2

Optimization Model

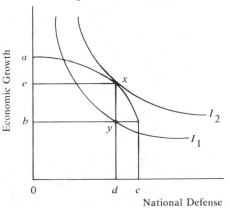

trade-off relationship, less growth versus more defense, and vice versa. Since *c* is the maximum level of defense achievable—and it can be attained with only half of the resources—allocation of more than half of the resources to defense will only decrease growth, without any corresponding increase in defense performance.

The possibilities of converting available resources into performance results, and hence the trade-off among the results themselves, are essentially matters for technical analysis. However, the choice among the achievable alternatives depends upon the relative preferences of policy-makers for the two goals. Imagine that such preferences are known and that they can be expressed in terms of an "indifference curve," an array of combinations of levels of growth and defense among which the policy-maker is indifferent. Such curves are shown as I_1 and I_2 in Figure 5-2. Every point on I_2 is preferred to every point on I_1 since each point on the higher curve involves higher performance of one or both policy goals as compared to some point on the lower one. I_2 is the highest indifference curve touched by the performance possibility curve *ac*. The two touch at point *x*, which represents a combination of *e* growth and *d* defense. Hence, this combination is the *optimal* choice of policy alternatives under the technical conditions, resource constraints, and policy preferences assumed here. The optimization analysis leads to the conclusion that about 70% of the resources should be allocated to economic growth and 30% to national defense. It can be easily seen that policy-makers' preferences could change so as to alter the optimal combination of performance levels, and in either direction. Also, technical conditions may change so that more or less of either goal might be obtained with the same amount of resources. If more of either can be obtained without loss of the other, the frontier of performance alternatives will shift out, and higher indifference curves—representing situations preferred to those represented along I_2—may become relevant. Similarly, if the total volume of resources available should increase, the entire frontier will shift out, and higher performance levels of one or both variables can be achieved.

The optimization model is a useful analytical construct, and sophisticated techniques exist for applying it to the solution of highly complex real problems. It is, however, at best only a very partial model of the public policy process. Its usefulness is limited by its stringent analytical requirements: first, that rather precise relationships between resource inputs and performance results be known, or at least hypothesized; second, that policy-makers' preferences are assumed to be known or discoverable. Both of these requirements are useful guides to systematic analysis, and an attempt to meet them should clarify rather than obscure the nature of the decision process. The principal limitation of the optimization model, however, is its limited scope. It takes no account of the way in which policy goals are articulated, alternatives proposed, and preferences discovered. Thus, optimization does not really describe a social decision process at all. The model is an intellectual construction, setting forth the formal relationship among given conditions.

However, the framing of alternatives in optimization terms may contribute to the discussion and clarification of issues and hence provide a valuable input into a larger social and political process through which public policy is formed. Furthermore, once a social decision has taken place, it may well be analyzable in these terms.

It perhaps should be mentioned that optimization analysis is peculiarly the province of members of the technostructure. However, it should not therefore be assumed that an extension of technostructure dominance throughout society, even if such should occur, would increase the descriptive accuracy of the optimization model as a description of social processes. On the contrary, although the presence of larger numbers of technically sophisticated people in policy-related roles certainly increases the use of optimization techniques and models—with, hopefully, general benefits of improved analysis and avoidance of suboptimal outcomes—technocrats are no less likely than other people to become caught up in conflicts of ideology and procedure, and hence to escape from the elegant requirements of the models into the rough and tumble of reality.

Incrementalism

The incrementalist approach, which offers a sharp contrast to the optimization principle, states that policy formation proceeds by small steps, "successive limited comparisons," or—with only a trace of humor—"the science of muddling through." As expressed by its strongest exponent, Charles E. Lindblom, incrementalism involves "A denial of the general validity of two assumptions implicit in most of the literature of policy making. The first is that public policy problems can best be solved by attempting to understand them; the second is that there exists sufficient agreement to provide adequate criteria for choosing among possible alternative policies."[8] Lindblom not only denies the validity of these two propositions; he argues that the necessary and even desirable method of policy formation is, in fact, experimentation and modification through small changes rather than comprehensive analysis in search of global optima. Aaron Wildavsky, another leading incrementalist, places a greater emphasis than Lindblom on formal analytical procedures, but is no less critical of comprehensive optimization techniques, particularly as applied to governmental budgeting. As he sums it up: "All of the obstacles . . ., such as lack of talent, theory, and data, may be summed up in a single statement: *no one knows hoe to do [it]*. Another way of putting it would be to say that many know what [it] should be like in general, but no one knows what it should be in any particular case.[9]

---

[8] Albert O. Hirschman and Charles E. Lindblom, "Economic Development, Research and Development, Policy Making: Some Converging Views," *Behavioral Science* (April 1962), pp. 211ff.

[9] Aaron Wildavsky, "Rescuing Policy Analysis from PPBS," in *Public Expenditures and Policy Analysis*, ed. Robert Haveman and Julius Margolis, (Chicago: Markham Publishing

EXHIBIT 5-1

Rational-Comprehensive	Successive Limited Comparisons
(1a) Clarification of values or objectives distinct from and usually prerequisite to empirical analysis of alternative policies.	(1b) Selection of value goals and empirical analysis of the needed action are not distinct from one another but are closely intertwined.
(2a) Policy formulation is therefore approached through means-end analysis: First the ends are isolated, then the means to achieve them are sought.	(2b) Since means and ends are not distinct, means-end analysis is often inappropriate or limited.
(3a) The test of a "good" policy is that it can be shown to be the most appropriate means to desired ends.	(3b) The test of a "good" policy is typically that various analysts find themselves directly agreeing on a policy (without their agreeing that it is the most appropriate means to an agreed objective).
(4a) Analysis is comprehensive; every important relevant factor is taken into account.	(4b) Analysis is drastically limited: i) Important possible outcomes are neglected. ii) Important alternative potential policies are neglected. iii) Important affected values are neglected.
(5a) Theory is often heavily relied upon.	(5b) A succession of comparisons greatly reduces or eliminates reliance on theory.

Source: Charles E. Lindblom, "The Science of 'Muddling Through,' " *Public Administration Review,* XIX, No. 2 (1959), p. 81.

The contrast between incrementalism and formal optimization is summarized in Exhibit 5-1, adapted from one of Lindblom's early expositions. Two essential points are emphasized: first, that means and ends are not really distinct, but interrelated; and second, that choices can in fact be made only among a group of fairly close-by, well-defined alternatives. For example, referring back to Figure 5-2, if the policy-making apparatus had previously settled on some point (such as y) along I_1, the lower indifference curve, an improvement could be made by a shift to *any point* above I_1. The preferred alternative might represent an increase of economic growth or national defense, or both, but it need not lie in the "direction" of x, the analytical optimum.

The incrementalist thesis is that the policy-formation process *does and should* take the form of the sequential discovery, appraisal, and movement

Company, 1970), p. 467. His general viewpoint is presented in *The Politics of the Budgetary Process* (Boston: Little, Brown, 1964), and also in *Toward a Radical Incrementalism* (Washington, D.C.: American Enterprise Institute for Public Policy Research, December 1965). For a comprehensive critique of optimization techniques in government budgeting and planning, see Leonard Merewitz and Stephen H. Sosnick, *The Budget's New Clothes* (Chicago: Markham Publishing Company, 1971).

toward points superior to *y* and that for this purpose a global analysis within a framework of optimization theory and techniques may be useless, if not positively harmful. Lindblom contrasts "the classical way of fragmenting a problem"—i.e., dividing it into a "neat hierarchical structure, trying to find logical subparts which can be treated somewhat separately, with some kind of summary overview of their interrelation"—with other methods of problem solving, "such as fragmenting it in *time*. You can pick up a piece of the problem and cope with it, and then cope (as your *next* problem) with the adverse consequences, some expected and some unexpected, of your solution to the first step; and at the third step, you cope with adverse consequences of your second step, etc. . . . Practical experience shows that this is perhaps the most common way we actually go about fragmenting overly large problems into manageable ones."[10]

Against a background of historical observation, it is impossible to quarrel with the incremental model as a description of the policy-formation process. At the same time, either as a scientific proposition or as a guide to appropriate decision-making approaches, incrementalism has serious limitations. It offers no basis for predicting *which* of many possible incremental changes will be given careful consideration, or which *one* of them will be chosen. As a guide to action, incrementalism must be supplemented by some type of more extensive qualitative analysis in order to determine even the direction in which improvements lie. In a sense, the incrementalist critique of optimization analysis is simply a sophisticated application of the ancient adage: The best is enemy of the good. Incrementalists stress that nearby and achievable "goods" may be preferable to remote and uncertain "bests."

Power and Bargaining

The ability to control resources, withstand adverse developments, and influence the opinion and behavior of others clearly varies among individuals and groups within society. These differences give rise to differences in social and economic power. Most of the "political" models of the public policy process place heavy stress on the identity, strength, and goals of various power centers within society, and on processes of conflict, bargaining, and cooperation among them.

Both the "exploitation model" and the "technostructure model" of the management-society relationship, discussed in Chapter 2, are simple "power models" of the social system. More complex and detailed analyses stress the distinction between formal power centers—as, for example, the various units of government—and the specific constituencies, groups, and individuals who possess effective power, including the power to influence government itself.

The notion that public policy-making and the process of government are to be explained primarily in terms of the interaction of identifiable groups, each

---

[10] Charles E. Lindblom, *Proceedings,* Conference on Management and Public Policy, School of Management, State University of New York at Buffalo, May 20-22, 1972, p. 51.

possessing some elements of social power, was first enunciated by Arthur Bentley.[11] This thesis is now an important, but highly controversial, element in modern political science. It is generally acknowledged that many different interest and pressure groups exist within society, that particular individuals may belong to more than one such group, and that intergroup equilibrium can be established through processes of bargaining and compromise. The key analytical questions are (1) whether the *relative* power of various groups can be accurately assessed, and hence the eventual outcome predicted, *ex ante;* and (2) whether the *process* of communication, negotiation, and bargaining is more important than the basic power positions in any event. A further and more general issue is the acceptability of both conflicts and bargains involving particular groups within the general framework of the governmental structure and the social system as a whole.[12]

The essence of power is the ability to impose penalties or to distribute rewards. Hence, the appraisal of *relative* power lies in a comparison of the penalizing and rewarding abilities of conflicting groups. If we visualize a closed system containing two competing groups and no third parties, then the (relative) gains of one party can be described as the (relative) losses of the other. When third parties (including the "rest" of society) are present, however, they may be brought into the bargaining process if either or both of the parties directly engaged can establish a penalty-reward relationship with them.

Suppose there are two manufacturing industries, one of which is the supplier of materials for the other. Management in the supplying industry anticipates that foreign imports may lead to reduction in prices and profits and therefore requests tariff protection from the government. The consuming industry reacts by opposing such protection. It is conceivable that there are such conspicuous differences in size, profitability, importance for national defense, or political recognition between the two industries that their relative power positions would be obvious and the outcome easily predictable. On the other hand, it is possible that their initial power positions would be evenly balanced, and the status quo left undisturbed. However, if the supplying-industry management can convince its labor force, their union representa-

---

[11] Arthur F. Bentley, *The Process of Government: A Study of Social Pressures* (Chicago: University of Chicago Press, 1908; republished by Principia Press, 1949); see also David B. Truman, *The Governmental Process: Political Interests and Public Opinion* (New York: Alfred A. Knopf, Inc., 1963).

[12] Interesting case studies of bargaining processes in public policy related to business and economic affairs are: Stewart Macaulay, *Law and the Balance of Power: The Automobile Manufacturers and Their Dealers* (New York: Russell Sage Foundation, 1966); Stephen K. Bailey, *Congress Makes a Law: The Story Behind the Employment Act of 1946* (New York: Columbia University Press, 1950); Daniel P. Moynihan, *The Politics of a Guaranteed Income* (New York: Random House, Inc., 1973); Raymond A. Bauer, Ithiel de Sola Pool, and Lewis Anthony Dexter, *American Business and Public Policy,* 2nd ed. (New York: Atherton Press, 1972). For a comprehensive survey of literature and issues relating to corporate power, see E. M. Epstein, "Dimensions of Corporate Power," Pts. I and II, *California Management Review,* No. 2, pp. 9-23, and No. 4, pp. 32-47.

tives, and elected political representatives in its operating locations that import pressure on prices and profits threatens their own interest and welfare, a new element may be added to the situation: A coalition of interests increasing the power of one side relative to the other. Of course, the other industry may respond in a similar fashion, or may initiate other empowering moves—such as direct lobbying, public relations efforts, and so forth—in order to alter the situation.

The importance of action and reaction among power centers has lead to an emphasis on communication and the bargaining *process* within political models of policy making. A bargain is a mutually acceptable division of contributions and rewards among negotiating parties. Figure 5-3 is a schematic illustration of a bargaining relationship. Suppose that there are two negotiating parties, Yin and Yang, and each has his own particular performance goals (economic, social, environmental, or whatever).[13] Each has the power to reduce the other's goal achievement to zero, but at the sacrifice of all goal achievement for himself as well; in this sense, the two parties possess equal and ultimate *power* over each other. Point *a* represents the minimum level of Yin's performance goals, the level that he would insist on achieving before he would be willing to accept *any* goal achievement for Yang. Similarly, point *a'* is the minimum goal achievement level for Yang. However, if Yin achieves his goals to the level of *a*, Yang will insist upon goal achievement to a level of *b*. Yin will in turn require level *c*, Yang will require a corresponding level *d*, and so forth. If all of these goal-achievement levels are *possible* within the environment, the result is an eventual equilibrium at point *x*, where each has attained a level of goal satisfaction compatible with that attained by the other. The two goal levels at *x* do not, of course, have to be the same or even of the same character. Yin's values could be primarily economic, for example, and Yang's could be related to social status, educational opportunity, or whatever. The point is that Yin and Yang simply find some mutually satisfactory combination of their respective goals.

The benign solution illustrated in Figure 5-3 is, of course, only one of many possible cases. Depending upon the shapes of the bargaining curves and the initial conditions assumed, situations can be illustrated in which zero benefits for both parties, perpetual instability, or utter perversity (no basis for agreement) results. Also, it is possible to integrate this type of analysis with the concept of performance-possibility frontier in the optimization model (see Figure 5-2). The bargaining functions then replace the policymaker's indifference curve as the determinant of policy choices among feasible alternatives. (Let national defense be Yin's goal and economic growth be Yang's, and the analysis falls directly into place.)

This simple model of bargaining makes no allowance for the importance of

---

[13] The facts that Yin and Yang, although antithetical principles, are intertwined and that both are essential for human life have inspired our choice here. Most social bargains do take place among parties who cannot, in fact, do without each other.

FIGURE 5-3

Bargaining Model

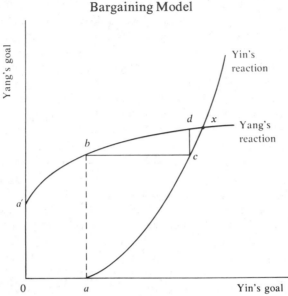

communications techniques, calendar time, interpersonal relationships, and adaptive changes in both knowledge and goals during the bargaining process. When important and well-organized interest groups negotiate in public over major policy issues, such elements of the process may be paramount. Certainly, they will be conspicuous, as the case studies listed in footnote 12 illustrate in fascinating detail. The important point for present purposes is that any and all such elements are of potential importance in the social process of policy formation.

The virtue of power and bargaining models, whether naive or complex, is that they take explicit account of a simple fact about the public policy process: The particular interests favoring or opposing a policy proposal, and their ability to inflict penalties or distribute rewards to others, have considerable impact on the direction, character, and speed of policy developments. At the same time, in a large and complex society, two conditions simultaneously hold: first, many groups and interests have the ability to impose heavy costs on the rest of society in the short run; and second, the variety and flexibility of groups is so great that almost any particular power center could be neutralized or eliminated by proper actions and coalitions among other parties. The resulting paradox is that although many groups and interests appear to possess very substantial power over the rest of society in the short run, their ability to exert such power for their own narrow purposes in the long run is severely limited. Hence, forces of compromise and cooperation significantly mitigate the impact of short-run power on the evolution of public policy. Indeed, effective use of power with respect to any major policy issue almost inevitably involves the establishment of large coalitions in which individual power positions have already been subsumed under patterns of compromise and cooperation. Hence, a concept of group equilibrium, in which multiple power centers are balanced against each other in a complex of coalitions and networks, comes to replace simple models of power and bargaining in a comprehensive analysis.

AN INSTITUTIONAL-SYSTEMS MODEL

The elements of an institutional-systems model of the public policy process, which provides a framework for integrating the three previous conceptions and many others as well, is sketched in Figure 5-4.[14] In this model, the primary initiative in identifying issues for public policy consideration is lodged in society at large and in its various constituent elements. (This aspect of the model is further discussed in the following chapter.) Policy-making actions take place within the constitutional and governmental system, a set of institutional relationships of long duration and subject only to incremental adaptation within the context of any particular analysis. The process of *explicit* public policy formation—i.e., the development of public policy with respect to some particular issue or problem—is comprehensively outlined, beginning with (1) the initial specification of the policy agenda item and continuing through (2) the analysis phase (whether comprehensive or incremental), (3) decision and establishment of an implementation structure, and (4) implementation experience. The explicit process with respect to any particular issue leads to evaluation and feedback within each of the major action units (i.e., society and government), and also with respect to the process itself.

The institutional systems model accommodates the optimization approach as an important element in the analysis phase and also as a form of evaluation and feedback at both the society and government levels. Incrementalism is, of course, acknowledged in the relative permanence of the governmental and statutory system and in the emphasis upon institutional and sequential steps within the process itself. Power and bargaining play important roles at both the society and government levels, and both with respect to the general and continuing structure of the system and the explicit process of policy formation concerning any particular issue.

The institutional systems model also permits recognition of an important aspect of public policy not readily included in other conceptions. Consideration of new policy issues and the decision to "do something" about them often leads to action in the form of institutional change rather than, or in addition to, specific direct treatment of the problem or area. The first sign of

---

[14] This particular formulation is derived from lecture presentations by Professors Joseph Shister and Philip Ross.

FIGURE 5-4

Insitutional Systems Model of the Public Policy Process

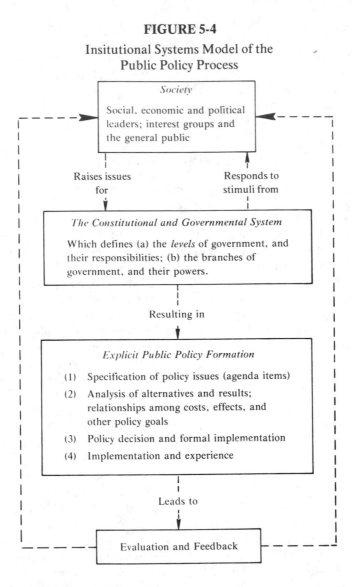

recognition of a new problem or task within any organization is usually the appointment of a committee to study it. Not only is a similar short-run response common to public bodies as well, but, more important, the eventual public policy decision may be to create a new and continuing entity to take primary responsibility for public policy development and implementation within the particular area.

This aspect of the policy process is epitomized by the establishment of the Federal Administrative Agencies—the ICC, FTC, etc.—under broad congressional guidelines. These entities, at the time of their creation, represented new public policy responses. Thereafter they became part of the governmental system itself, generating pressures for or against change in society at large and shaping explicit public policy with respect to issues within their spheres of responsibility. Further, institutional innovations not only alter the basic system itself and generate feedback effects through their own operations; they also generate more fundamental feedbacks as examples of institutional alternatives that might be applied to other emerging issues. Thus, for example, there is a kind of "genetic" connection between the FTC and NLRB, with the structure and function of the latter—including relationships with the court system and with the relevant executive departments (justice and labor, respectively) and the presidency—modeled considerably on that of the former. Similarly, the long unsatisfactory history of the ICC with respect to the railroads has cast a permanent shadow over detailed regulation as a policy-implementation device in entirely unrelated areas of economic and social life.[15]

A second feature of the institutional-systems model is its emphasis on policy development as a recurring, sequential process in which there is fundamentally no beginning, middle, or end. Indeed, the appraisal of policy actions on the basis of experience, and the resulting reformulation and adaptation, probably accounts for a much larger share of total policy-making activity—and certainly a larger share of the total impact of policy—than the explicit consideration of policy issues in new areas. This emphasis on interlinkages and internal adjustments increases the complexity of the model and reduces the precision with which it can be applied. However, since both of these losses in formal elegance increase the model's descriptive accuracy, they are probably justified for our purposes.

A final feature of the institutional-systems model, and one which is no accident in the present context, is that it readily accommodates the interpenetrating systems model of management and society sketched in Chapter 2. In effect, this model of the public policy process is a specific articulation of some aspects of the elementary concept of "society" presented there. Hence, we may visualize private business management as overlapping and interlinked with each element in the institutional systems model—with society as a whole; with the governmental structure in general; with those particular policy formation situations in which individual managers become directly involved; and with the processes of evaluation and feedback. Thus, the institutional systems model provides the comprehensive framework for our basic conception of management-society interaction through the public policy process.

[15] See Louis M. Kohlmeier, Jr., *The Regulators: Watchdog Agencies and the Public Interest* (New York: Harper & Row, Inc., 1969); Robert Chatov, "Independent Regulatory Agency Behavior" (mimeographed paper, 1972); and the various reports of the Ralph Nader organization relating to specific regulatory agencies.

SUMMARY

The widely shared and generally acknowledged principles directing or controlling social activity within organized societies constitute public policy. Such policies need not be universally accepted, or even known, but they are reflected in the actions and inactions of governments in a variety of ways. Public policy may take the form of implicit norms and standards that form the background of formal governmental activity, explicit governmental prohibitions or requirements, public programs, or guidelines and stimuli for private and individual response. The substance of public policy is affected as much by acceptance and implementation as by formal enactment or statement of principle.

There are many concepts of the policy-making process in large, complex societies. The optimization model stresses the rational selection of means to accomplish predetermined goals. Incrementalism stresses the lack of comprehensive information and knowledge and the importance of gradual adaptation to changes over time. Power and bargaining models stress the identity and relative strength of various interests and groups involved in particular policy decisions, and the sequential processes of communication and negotiation. The institutional-systems model provides a framework within which these and other conceptions of the public policy process may be integrated and provides a particularly useful basis for our analysis of management-society interpenetration.

CHAPTER SIX

The Public Policy Agenda

SHAPING THE POLICY AGENDA

The previous chapter discussed some general characteristics of public policy and the diverse ways in which such policies can be affirmed and articulated—from implicit acceptance to rhetorical suggestion to detailed specification. Here we raise different questions: Which areas of social life are included, and which excluded, from the purview of public policy? How are areas and issues added to, or subtracted from, the policy agenda?

Answers to these questions can be found in sources as varied as the most ancient philosophers and the most recent opinion polls. A long tradition in philosophy and law deals with the "proper" function of government, and minimum requirements usually include provision for national defense and a system of law and justice. An opposite view is suggested by Moynihan: "There are no social interests about which the national government does not have some policy or other, simply by virtue of the indirect influences of programs nominally directed to other areas."[1] Of course, the proposition that public policy covers "everything" is truistically accurate in the sense that the omission of any particular matter from the public policy agenda is in itself the result of a policy decision, implicit or explicit. More importantly, however, Moynihan is undoubtedly correct in that the agenda of public policy in our society includes an enormous number of issues and areas by explicit decision and most others by secondary impact.

Mere recognition of this fact, whether it is welcomed or not, has served to shift interest away from philosophical debate about the "proper" function of government and toward analysis of the ways in which issues are brought onto the public policy agenda and the process by which an agenda item is defined and recognized. Four elements play critical roles: public opinion, interest and pressure groups, social and political leadership, and technical expertise.

Public Opinion

Public opinion has been defined by Key as "those opinions held by private persons which governments find it prudent to heed."[2] He emphasizes that "consensus does not have to prevail" and that there are many "special publics" within the "general public." Further, there are differences in the salience of issues, the intensity with which opinions are held, and on the stability of opinion over time. There are also areas of public opinion—such as opinions about products, life styles, or religious practices—that have little or nothing to do with public policy in any formal sense. The point, however, is that general concern with some aspect of social life and a belief that collective action should be undertaken to improve or correct it must be embraced by some substantial and influential segment of society before that aspect of life can be brought into the public policy agenda. Note that there is a trade-off between numbers and salience-intensity in this regard. Issues having little (but some) importance to large numbers of citizens may be equally prominent on the agenda with those prossessing great salience for vocal minorities.

Interest and Pressure Groups

Characteristics and interests shared among various members of society, but not by all of them, give rise to the formation of groups—formal and informal, large and small, highly specialized and general purpose. The role of such groups was mentioned in the preceding chapter in discussing the distribution of power in society and the establishment of intergroup equilibrium

[1] Daniel P. Moynihan, "Policy vs. Program in the '70's," *The Public Interest,* No. 20 (Summer 1970), p. 93.

[2] V. O. Key, Jr., *Public Opinion and American Democracy* (New York: Alfred A. Knopf, Inc., 1967), p. 14.

through bargaining. Here we draw attention to the role of interest and pressure groups in bringing particular issues and concerns onto the public policy agenda.

Groups engaged in the political process are often said to represent "vested interests"—i.e., private or personal benefits arising as a matter of right or custom. Although this term is often used in a perjorative sense, such interests may, in fact, be entirely legitimate and socially acceptable. Indeed, the observation that various groups within society utilize the public policy process in order to further their own interests, whether literally "vested" or not, is simply factual; it implies neither praise nor criticism of the particular interests involved or methods used.

There is, however, a distinct difference in the role of interest and pressure groups in bringing particular issues to light, so that public opinion about them can develop, on the one hand, and their role in influencing the policy-making process with respect to specific substantive matters, on the other. In our own society, permeated by the activities of mass communications media, virtually any group of people can manage to get a certain amount of public attention focused on their particular enthusiasms or concerns if they choose to do so. However, in actually bringing specific issues into sufficient prominence that they can be recognized as matters for public consideration, and then in achieving specified policy results, the importance of size, financial backing, continuity of objectives and leadership, and other organizational strengths becomes greatly increased. Even the basic validity of group-theory approaches, including the likelihood of group cohesiveness without coercion and the ability of groups to identify and act upon their own interests, has been seriously questioned, most notably by Mancur Olson.[3]

Leadership

Leadership by key individuals and groups is perhaps the most conspicuous feature of the process of public policy formation when it is observed in a "live" context. Personal characteristics and styles often seem to dominate the substantive issues under debate. Sometimes leaders rise to prominence simply because of their association with some salient issue; in other instances, established leadership elements identify themselves with evolving viewpoints.[4] Whatever the particular circumstance, there is serious analytical controversy as to the real significance of leadership factors in shaping

[3] Mancur Olson, *The Logic of Collective Action* (Cambridge, Mass.: Harvard University Press, 1971). The standard modern reference to the role of groups in public policy formation is David B. Truman, *The Governmental Process: Political Interests and Public Opinion* (New York: Alfred A. Knopf, Inc., 1951).

[4] Classic analyses of the role of leadership in society are: C. Wright Mills, *The Power Elite* (New York: Oxford University Press, 1956) and William G. Domhoff, *Who Rules America?* (Englewood Cliffs, N.J.: Prentice-Hall, Inc., 1967). Of special relevance here is William G. Domhoff, "How the Power Elite Sets National Goals," in *National Priorities,* ed. Kan Chen (San Francisco: San Francisco Press, 1970).

public policy. The traditional analysis of political history lays great stress on the role of outstanding individuals and specialized groups in the historical process. A broader social science approach stresses the importance of long-range historical developments and the evolution of widely held opinions. A reasonable compromise position holds that leadership elements exert considerable impact on the *timing* of public policy initiatives, on the particular form in which issues are identified (e.g., "school integration" or "forced busing"), and on the short-run pattern of developments. At the same time, the widespread recognition of "problem" phenomena is essential to any significant change in the public policy agenda or in the direction of policy with respect to specific issues. Ralph Nader could scarcely have become a national figure overnight if many automobile drivers had not already suspected that their vehicles were "unsafe at any speed."

Technical Expertise

Technical expertise, with regard to public policy issues, involves understanding the causes and characteristics of public policy problems and of methods of dealing with them.[5] The importance of expertise is perhaps best indicated by famous cases of its absence. Every schoolboy knows that malaria was so named for the "bad air" that was presumed to be its cause; many centuries elapsed before the role of the malaria parasite, and of the mosquito in its transmission, were clearly understood. Similar errors of technical analysis attribute poverty to a lack of moral worth on the part of the poor, individual vitality or lethargy to skin pigmentation, and so forth. For social conditions as well as physical ones, correct diagnosis is generally an essential preliminary to effective treatment.

Technical expertise is also vital for distinguishing between "problems"—that is, situations about which something presumably can be done—and the "nature of things," about which nothing can be done. Until well into the present century, severe and unpredictable fluctuations in the level of overall economic activity—production, employment, wages, and prices—were thought to be inherent characteristics of economic life. These cycles were regarded as "natural" phenomena, comparable to weather and earthquakes. The effects of these cycles could be aggravated or dampened by a variety of public policy actions, and their human impact could be mitigated by charity; but it was not seriously contemplated that they might be avoided altogether.

By contrast, the notion that severe macro-economic instability can be subjected to control is now as commonly accepted as the association of the mosquito with malaria. Both debate and research continue as to the role of particular techniques in macro-economic stabilization and the relative desirability of other macro-economic goals (such as long-run growth, changes in income distribution, or international economic relationships) in

---

[5] For a penetrating analysis, see Guy Benveniste, *The Politics of Expertise* (Berkeley, Cal.: The Glendessary Press, 1972).

addition to the goal of stability. However, the notion that instability is not an inevitable condition but instead a "problem," capable of diagnosis and solution, is now almost universally accepted—not only among economists, but also among policy-makers, businessmen, workers, and private citizens. Distinguishing between "problems" and natural phenomena, and correctly diagnosing the problems themselves, is the powerful role of technical expertise in the formation of public policy.

The second role of technical expertise is the development of solutions to problems once they have been identified. As the incremental model of the policy process emphasizes, the availability of solutions is a critical determinant of the position of particular issues on the public policy agenda. For example, if macro-economic instability could be avoided simply by public exhortation, it would no doubt be universally considered a desirable policy goal to be achieved. On the other hand, if the conversion of the entire economy to a centrally planned regime were required in order to eliminate major fluctuations in production and employment, a substantial majority of citizens might feel that the end did not justify the means. Hence, the availability and impact of a variety of intermediate stabilization policies has a great deal to do with the acceptance of macro-economic stabilization as a significant national goal.

THE CURRENT POLICY AGENDA

The basic framework for the public policy agenda in the United States is set forth in the Preamble to the Constitution:

> . . . Form a more perfect union,
> Establish justice,
> Ensure domestic tranquility,
> Provide for the common defense,
> Promote the general welfare, and
> Secure the blessings of liberty . . .

These elementary and sweeping notions set the direction for long-term policy development. The early Presidents and Congresses did not, however, see the orderly extension and articulation of these principles as their primary tasks. Rather, formal public policy evolved at uneven speeds and in diverse directions in response to specific historical situations and developments. In fact, comprehensive surveys and analyses of the agenda of national policy—other than in such documents as the State of the Union messages of the Presidents—have only recently become more or less commonplace.

Goals for Americans

Current awareness of the nature of public policy and the need for a broad survey of national goals and tasks that would form the agenda for policy consideration can be dated from President Eisenhower's appointment of a

Commission on National Goals in 1959.[6] This committee's report, *Goals for Americans*, has become the basic document for subsequent analyses of the policy agenda up to the present time. Extracts from this document are presented in the Appendix to this chapter.

According to the commission:

> The paramount goal of the United States . . . is to guard the rights of the individual. It is . . . a mighty vision, . . . an even broader and bolder declaration than those who made it knew.[7]

The relatively brief commission report was accompanied by a series of discussion papers in which substantive issues and policy alternatives in various specific areas were developed in more detail. Although the report itself strongly emphasized the role of individual initiative and responsibility, as opposed to government action, in the achievement of goals, the background essays inevitably stressed the interaction of citizens and groups—and the role of society as a whole—within the public policy process. The publication of *Goals for Americans* was followed by several years of widespread, and sometimes heated, public discussion of the scope of the public policy agenda and the proper content of policy with respect to specific items. Some of the concrete proposals put forward were eventually incorporated in the Great Society programs of the Johnson Administration.

The next major survey of the agenda in its entirety occurred, however, in preparation for the presidential transition of 1968-69. *Agenda for the Nation*,[8] a volume of study papers organized by the Brookings Institution, avoided the sweeping rhetoric of the Eisenhower commission in favor of a problem-oriented analysis, with heavy stress on specific action alternatives. On the domestic front, *Agenda*—like *Goals*—gave a prominent place to improving the economic and social status of disadvantaged groups. It also provided a basic framework for the analysis of public policy within the overall budget and major programs of the federal government. Housing, crime, education, government management, and macro-economic stability were the special topics given primary consideration. (Foreign policy topics—which were accorded equal prominence in both *Goals* and *Agenda*—are not listed here in detail, although the growing importance of international *economic* relationships is reflected in their much greater prominence in the Brookings volume.) A third presidential report, *Toward Balanced Growth: Quantity*

---

[6] This priority position might have been occupied by Herbert Hoover, who appointed a Research Committee on Social Trends in the fateful month of September, 1929. That Committee, headed by the distinguished economist Wesley C. Mitchell, eventually produced a two-volume report that has not subsequently been matched for comprehensiveness or breadth of view. Unfortunately, since the document appeared in 1933, it seems to have rested almost unnoticed in the archives. See *Recent Social Trends,* Report of the President's Research Committee (New York: McGraw-Hill Book Company, 1933).

[7] The American Assembly, *Goals for Americans,* The Report of the President's Commission on National Goals (Englewood Cliffs, N.J.: Prentice-Hall, Inc., 1960).

[8] Kermit Gordon, ed., *Agenda for the Nation* (Washington, D.C.: The Brookings Institution, 1968).

with Quality, resulted from the work of a White House staff group under the direction of Daniel Patrick Moynihan in 1970.[9]

Analysis of the policy agenda and its component parts has now become a field of study in itself, and two major strands of analysis have developed. One of these deals with issues of theory and measurement, while the other—like the presidential studies mentioned above—focuses on the substantive content of national policy and the implicit priorities, or possible alternatives, reflected therein.

Theory and Measurement: Social Indicators

The social indicators approach to describing and analyzing the state of society and changes therein became prominent as a result of two major scholarly publications[10] and the issuance of a thin document, *Toward a Social Report,* by the U.S. Department of Health, Education and Welfare.[11] The thesis of this approach is that if there is to be any serious consideration of broad social policy goals and alternatives, evaluation of programs, and improvement in goal-achievement over time, then a rigorous attempt must be made to formulate explicit models and hypotheses and to measure performance results.

Toward a Social Report identifies seven major areas of social concern:

Health and illness
Social mobility
Physical environment
Income and poverty
Public order and safety
Learning, science and art
Participation and alienation

(Macro-economic issues are exluded in the presumption that measurement techniques and concepts in this area are well-developed; international issues are excluded by the scope of the project.) The study does not attempt to enunicate specific goals or policies relevant to any of these areas. Instead, the authors simply recognize these areas as prominent in current discussions of social conditions. There is an implicit assumption that social consensus exists as to the direction in which change might be desirable (i.e., a general consensus on the difference between "better" and "worse" conditions in each area),

---

[9] National Goals Research Staff, *Toward Balanced Growth: Quantity with Quality* (Washington, D.C.: U.S. Government Printing Office, 1970).

[10] Raymond A. Bauer, ed., *Social Indicators* (Cambridge, Mass.: Massachusetts Institute of Technology, 1966); see also Eleanor Sheldon and W. E. Moore, eds., *Indicators of Social Change* (New York: Russell Sage Foundation, 1968).

[11] United States Department of Health, Education and Welfare, *Toward a Social Report* (Washington, D.C.: U.S. Government Printing Office, 1969).

although no consensus might exist as to the desired pattern or rate of change, or to the priority to be attached to each area. The study raises a more limited, but logically prior, question: How can we appraise the present state of each area, and how would we *know* if the state were changing? Collections of data that might be utilized for this purpose are tentatively presented and appraised, and suggestions for improved analysis—regardless of the particular policy goals adopted—are set forth. Much more extensive data, but without the analytical discussion, have been provided in *Social Indicators, 1973.*[12]

The more scholarly studies extend the problem of observation and measurement of social performance to include the extremely difficult problem of specifying the complex system within which social performance occurs. The notion that the system may have "goals" is accepted without detailed analysis, and the authors concentrate on developing in detail the relationships among system structure, function, performance measurement, and goal achievement.[13]

National Priorities

The second major thread of development in recent years is the analysis of actual and potential policy areas and alternatives in terms of *national priorities.* This type of analysis has now become available from a wide variety of sources, but the two principal groups of semi-official contributions are the series of volumes called *Setting National Priorities*, an annual analysis (beginning with the 1971 budget) of the federal budget and its implication, prepared by a group of scholars at the Brookings Institution under the direction of Charles Schultze,[14] and several White House documents appearing during the early years of the Nixon administration.

The Brookings approach, as the title of the analysis suggests, focuses principally on the impact of federal expenditures on social and economic conditions, and particularly on the relative size and operating thrust of programs in particular areas—defense, education, health, poverty, and so forth. The basic concept involves "performance budgeting," an expansion of emphasis from the traditional budgetary questions—*"What objectives* should the federal government seek, and *how much money* should be assigned to each?"*—to include *"How* the objectives should be achieved . . ."

[12] Office of Management and Budget, Executive Office of the President, *Social Indicators 1973* (Social and Economic Statistics Administration, U.S. Department of Commerce).

[13] Important references in addition to those discussed here are: Leonard A. Lecht, *Goals, Priorities and Dollars: The Next Decade* (New York: The Free Press, 1966); Robert Theobald, ed., *Social Policies for America in The Seventies* (New York: Doubleday, 1968); Kan Chen, ed., *National Priorities* (San Francisco: San Francisco Press, 1970); and Richard Lambert, ed., "America's Most Challenging Objectives," *The Annals* (July, 1971), CCCXCVI.

[14] Charles L. Schultze, *et al., Setting National Priorities* (Washington, D.C.: The Brookings Institution, 1970, 1971, 1972, 1973). Subsequent quotations are from the 1972 volume, pp. 450, 464, and 458.

and the effectiveness of goal achievement within budgetary allocation categories. After three years of work—preceded by many years of actual involvement in the federal budgetary process itself—the Brookings staff concluded that "the annual budget process is increasingly ill-suited to the intelligent setting of national priorities." A more comprehensive approach, involving a longer time horizon, was proposed.

In general, the Brookings studies call attention to considerable expansion of government functions that has come about as a result of the broadened public policy objectives of the 1960s and the difficulties of implementation, management, and evaluation that have been encountered in these new programs. While arguing for serious attention to improved control systems and managerial methods within these activities, as well as improved analysis of the interrelationships *among* the major acitivities themselves, the Brookings authors stress techniques of policy implementation that should reduce the need for detailed and comprehensive public sector management.

The pursuit of policy goals through the encouragement of desired patterns of behavior on the part of private organizations, both business and nonprofit, rather than through the establishment and operation of wholly public programs, receives strong support. They note: "There are two principal means by which the federal government could try to influence the behavior of individuals and institutions: by regulation, and by changing the incentives that individuals and institutions face. . . . The more traditional approach has been to change behavior by regulation. . . . The regulatory approach, however, has often proved inefficient and ineffective. . . . Hence, in many areas it would be preferable to de-emphasize the regulatory approach in favor of creating incentives for desirable behavior." The need for experimentation, in designing both programs and incentives, and for the appraisal of experiments when they are conducted is a recurrent theme. This experimentalist approach reflects, of course, the early and incomplete state of the theory-and-measurement developments previously discussed.

An even broader conception of the scope of public policy is reflected in *Toward Balanced Growth: Quantity with Quality* and in the annual *Economic Reports of the President* for 1970, 1971, and 1972. The 1970 White House study did not attempt to set forth a list of specific goals after the fashion of the Eisenhower Commission, nor did it attempt the more detailed performance evaluations suggested in *Toward a Social Report*. Instead, *Toward Balanced Growth* simply reflected a recognition that, in Moynihan's words, "there is no significant aspect of national life about which there is not likely to be a rather significant national policy. . . . Documents such as this report can become one of the essential channels by which the options before the Nation are presented in specific and comprehensive terms so that it becomes possible for a body of public opinion to form. . . ."[15] The areas for which policy issues were surveyed and potentially relevant data presented

[15] National Goals Research Staff, *Toward Balanced Growth*, pp. 6-9.

included: population, environment, education, basis science, technology assessment, consumerism, and a variety of problems of economic choice, including the choice between current consumption (or nonproduction) and growth. Discussion of national priorities in the several *Economic Reports* is, as would be expected, more narrowly focused. Yet, few areas of national life are unaffected by economic conditions, and in most critical areas of social policy—health, education, employment opportunities and housing, for example—economic factors constitute important, if not totally determining, aspects of each major problem situation.

The pervasive impact of government activity on all areas of economic activity is scarcely open to debate. Government expenditures (federal, state, and local) account for more than 20% of the total Gross National Product and a much larger portion of the GNP flows through government accounts—and often at more than one level of government—before reaching its final destination. Further, the economic impact of public policy—and particularly of federal government policy—is by no means confined to areas of specific budget expenditure. On the contrary, federal policy with respect to money supply and interest rates may have powerful impact on the level and pattern of private investment; federal loan and guarantee programs virtually determine the amount and type of new residential construction; the character of government-sponsored scientific and research activity may importantly determine the rate and direction of technological change and industrial development; and the mere expansion or contraction of government activity at one location or another may be the principal determinant of local levels of employment, wages, and business activity. Hence, in the economic sphere the impact of public policy on the operation of the entire society is clearly observed, and the trade-offs among policy goals and techniques are sharply drawn.

Recognition of the pervasive impact of federal policy upon economic life has led to the realization that, through the process of public policy formation, national policy-makers are, in a sense, "budgeting the Gross National Product." This point of view was extended to application in the 1970 *Economic Report* in the following terms: "We have placed the Nation's larger decisions in the context of a picture of the total resources available and the competing claims upon them. . . . The purpose of the analysis is to help everyone observe the discipline of keeping claims and plans within the limits of our capacity, and to make sure that excessive claims do not prevent us from achieving our most important goals. . . . Our problem, in short will be to choose wisely to do with our output and incomes."[16]

In their 1971 report, the Council of Economic Advisers analyzed the total usage of the GNP in ten functional categories, referred to as the "demands upon the national output." These categories, along with the slightly

[16] *Economic Report of the President* (Washington, D.C.: U.S. Government Printing Office, 1970), p. 4.

overlapping list of policy concerns in *Toward a Social Report*, completely cover the initial set of domestic policy issues originally set forth in *Goals for Americans*. The council does not argue that there are, or even should be, specific public policy goals with respect to the distribution of the GNP among these, or any other, categories of expenditure. Their presentation does, however, demonstrate that certain patterns of change—which may be taken to reflect implicit or effective priorities—can be detected even at this gross level of analysis. In particular, the shares of economic product devoted to education and manpower training, health, general government, and business investment increased over the period 1955-69, while the shares of basic necessities, defense, and new housing tended to decline. Further, the expansion of government expenditures and activity was clearly an important element in the aggregate expansion of input and output in some of these areas.

NEW DIRECTIONS

Formal and systematic analysis of the policy-making process and the public policy agenda is a relatively recent innovation, and new concepts and contributions to this activity are appearing from diverse sources and in many forms. Certainly the processes of formal goal setting and empirical investigation now underway for a couple of decades will be carried forward in the future. As a result, new policy-making mechanisms and concepts will undoubtedly evolve.

One current institutional proposal involves the establishment of a National Goals Institute or a Council of Social Advisers, comparable to the Council of Economic Advisers, probably within the Executive Office of the President. According to Arjay Miller, one of its strongest proponents, the tasks of such an agency would be, first, to project the magnitude of future increases in national output; second, to project the cost of present and contemplated programs and activities, public and private, including "the enormous cost of providing schools, hospitals, roads, productive facilities, etc., to keep up with projected population growth. . . ."; third, to "project the cost of attaining generally recognized goals over the next 10 years"; and, fourth, to estimate by subtraction "the 'gap' between the total cost of our goals and our ability to pay."[17]

Although the difficulty of these tasks—both the statement of the goals and the estimations of resources available and costs—is not to be underestimated, it appears likely that this proposal will be adopted in some form over the coming years. In 1973, a new National Commission on Critical Choices for Americans (directly analogous to the earlier Eisenhower Commission) was established as part of the preparations for the National Bicentennial.

On the conceptual side, the development of "social indicators" has now

---

[17] Arjay Miller, "A Proposal for a National Goals Institute," in *National Priorities*, ed. Kan Chen (San Francisco: San Francisco Press, 1970), pp. 27-32.

become a widespread activity in this and other countries, and this activity is almost certain to bear fruit in the near future. The most important recent innovation is the concept of "Net Economic Welfare," a term coined by Samuelson to describe original work by Nordhaus and Tobin. The essential idea is that the GNP, the most widely used and comprehensive measure of the total economic activity of society, fails to include a number of economic values—such as the value of leisure time and unpaid household services, for example—and also fails to take into account unpaid costs and disamentities, such as pollution and congestion. In estimating the NEW, an attempt is made to adjust the basic GNP figures upward and downward to bring these omitted values into consideration. According to Samuelson, NEW has grown much more slowly than GNP since 1950—in fact, NEW per capita, if that is an appropriate concept, must have declined substantially. He leaves the student with the question: "How much of GNP growth would you be willing to sacrifice to enhance the quality of life and NEW growth?"[18]

SUMMARY

The interaction of public opinion, interest and pressure groups, and leadership and technical expertise brings issues onto the public policy agenda. These forces work in a particular setting of historical development and experience, and in the context of particular economic and social environments—natural resources, population, state of technology, and legal and governmental system. It is difficult to explain, even after the fact, precisely how any single public policy issue came to be identified and acted upon.

Nevertheless, the formal identification of areas and issues for inclusion within the public policy agenda, the articulation of goals with respect to the selected areas, and the explicit consideration of policy alternatives is an ongoing and important activity within our society. The public at large may not yet realize how far and how quickly we have moved toward the evolution of a national consciousness and toward the explicit delineation of consensus, as well as specific disagreement, with respect to major social policy issues. At the same time, the formal theory of social processes is still in its infancy, and both theory and measurement techniques can be expected to evolve together during the coming decades. (By the year 2000, disputes as to whether social mobility is increasing or decreasing may seem as preposterous as disputes as to whether the size of the population is increasing or decreasing—an important subject of controversy around 1800—do today.)

Whatever our goals come to be, we may at least know more about how to accomplish them and be better able to tell whether we are accomplishing

[18] Paul A. Samuelson, *Economics,* 9th ed. (New York: McGraw-Hill Book Company, 1973), p. 196.

them or not. The simultaneous interaction of a changing, and probably expanding, agenda of public policy issues, increasingly well-defined goals, experimentation with a variety of implementation techniques, and an emphasis on measurement and evaluation—these form the scenario for public policy evolution over the coming decade. And an increasing awareness of this evolutionary process, probably leading to attempts to influence it in specific ways, will become characteristic not only of politicians and bureaucrats but of private business executives, public sector managers, and individual citizens as well.

Appendix:
Goals for Americans

INTRODUCTION

The paramount goal of the United States was set long ago. It is to guard the rights of the individual, to ensure his development, and to enlarge his opportunity. It is set forth in the Declaration of Independence drafted by Thomas Jefferson and adopted by the Continental Congress on July 4, 1776. The goals we here identify are within the framework of the original plan and are calculated to bring to fruition the dreams of the men who laid the foundation of this country.

They stated their convictions quite simply:

"We hold these truths to be self-evident, that all men are created equal, that they are endowed by their Creator with certain unalienable Rights, that among these are Life, Liberty, and the pursuit of Happiness. That to secure these rights, Governments are instituted among Men, deriving their just powers from the consent of the governed."

It was a mighty vision. In the echo of those fateful words can be heard the enrolling thunder of a new age. It was an even broader and bolder declaration than those who made it knew. Its soaring vision enabled our society to meet the trials of emerging nationhood. It placed the young republic securely behind the principle that every human being is of infinite worth. In time it led the nation out of the morass of human slavery. It inspires us still in the struggle against injustice.

To make this vision a reality, a framework of self-government was established nationally and in each state. It rested upon two fundamental principles—the election of representatives from among competing candidates, and the constitutional limitation of power of those elected.

The way to preserve freedom is to live it. Our enduring aim is to build a nation and help build a world in which every human being shall be free to

Extracted from *Goals for Americans*, Report of the President's Commission on National Goals (Englewood Cliffs, N.J.: Prentice-Hall, Inc., 1960).

develop his capacities to the fullest. We must rededicate ourselves to this principle and thereby strengthen its appeal to a world in political, social, economic and technological revolution.

This Report identifies goals and sets forth programs. It is directed to the citizens of this country, each of whom sets his own goals and seeks to realize them in his life, through private groups, and through various levels of government. Choices are hard, and costs heavy. They demand subordination of lesser goals to the greater. But the rewards are beyond calculation, for the future of our nation depends on the result.

At the same time, the United States cannot attain its goals alone, nor by offering the free world grudging alms or condescending leadership. We must lead, but in spirit of genuine partnership. Together, the free peoples of the world can develop unmatched strength and vindicate the mighty vision of the Declaration.

PART I: GOALS AT HOME

1. THE INDIVIDUAL

The status of the individual must remain our primary concern. All our institutions—political, social, and economic—must further enhance the dignity of the citizen, promote the maximum development of his capabilities, stimulate their responsible exercise, and widen the range and effectiveness of opportunities for individual choice.

2. EQUALITY

Vestiges of religious prejudice, handicaps to women, and, most important, discrimination on the basis of race must be recognized as morally wrong, economically wasteful, and in many respects dangerous. In this decade we must sharply lower these last stubborn barriers.

3. THE DEMOCRATIC PROCESS

The degree of effective liberty available to its people should be the ultimate test for any nation. Democracy is the only means so far devised by which a nation can meet this test. To preserve and perfect the democratic process in the United States is therefore a primary goal in this as in every decade.

4. EDUCATION

The development of the individual and the nation demand that education at every level and every discipline be strengthened and its effectiveness enhanced. New teaching techniques must continue to be developed. The increase in population and the growing complexity of the world add urgency.

Greater resources—private, corporate, municipal, state, and federal—must be mobilized. A higher proportion of the gross national product must be devoted to educational purposes. This is at once an investment in the individual, in the democratic process, in the growth of the economy and in the stature of the United States.

5. THE ARTS AND SCIENCES

Knowledge and innovation must be advanced on every front. In science we should allot a greater proportion of our total effort to basic research, first, to realize fully the rapidly unfolding opportunities to extend still further our understanding of the world, and second, to enrich applied science and technology so essential to the improvement of health, to economic growth, and to military power.

6. THE DEMOCRATIC ECONOMY

The economic system must be compatible with the political system. The centers of economic power should be as diffused and as balanced as possible. Too great concentrations of economic power in corporations, unions, or other organizations can lead to abuses and loss of the productive results of fair competition. Individuals should have maximum freedom in their choice of jobs, goods, and services.

7. ECONOMIC GROWTH

The economy should grow at the maximum rate consistent with primary dependence upon free enterprise and the avoidance of marked inflation. Increased investment in the public sector is compatible with this goal.

8. TECHNOLOGICAL CHANGE

Technological change should be promoted and encouraged as a powerful force for advancing our economy. It should be planned for and introduced with sensitive regard for any adverse impact upon individuals.

Education on a large scale is provided by many industrial firms for their personnel. Such activities combined with advance planning can minimize unemployment due to rapid technological change. Where re-employment within the industry is not possible, retraining must be carried out through vocational programs managed locally and financed through state and federal funds.

9. AGRICULTURE

The relative financial return to agriculture in the economy has deteriorated. The ultimate goal must be a supply-demand equilibrium to permit the market, with a fair return to farmers, to determine the manpower and capital committed to this sector of the economy. To avoid shock to the economy, this goal should be approached by gradual stages.

A separate problem concerns the 50 per cent of farmers who operate at subsistence levels and produce only 10 per cent of farm output. For them new opportunities must be found through training and through location of new industries in farm areas. During this decade non-farm jobs must be found—where possible locally—for about 1.5 million farm operators who now earn less than $1,500 a year.

10. LIVING CONDITIONS

We must remedy slum conditions, reverse the process of decay in the larger cities, and relieve the necessity for low-income and minority groups to concentrate there.

We should also seek solutions for haphazard suburban growth, and provide an equitable sharing of the cost of public services between central cities and suburbs. In many parts of the country, the goal should be a regional pattern which provides for a number of urban centers, each with its own industries, its own educational, cultural and recreational insitutions, and a balanced population of various income levels and backgrounds. The needs of a growing population for parks and recreation must be met.

11. HEALTH AND WELFARE

The demand for medical care has enormously increased. To meet it we must have more doctors, nurses, and other medical personnel. There should be more hospitals, clinics and nursing homes. Greater effectiveness in the use of such institutions will reduce over-all requirements. There is a heavy responsibility on the medical and public health professions to contribute better solutions.

Federal grants for the construction of hospitals should be continued and extended to other medical facilities. Increased private, state and federal support is necessary for training doctors.

Further efforts are needed to reduce the burden of the cost of medical care. Extension of medical insurance is necessary, through both public and private agencies.

PART II: GOALS ABROAD

Introduction

The basic foreign policy of the United States should be the preservation of its own independence and free institutions. Our position before the world should be neither defensive nor belligerent. We should cooperate with nations whose ideals and interests are in harmony with ours. We should seek to mitigate tensions, and search for acceptable areas of accommodation with opponents. The safeguarded reduction of armaments is an essential goal.

12. HELPING TO BUILD AN OPEN AND PEACEFUL WORLD

Foreign Trade Policy

The healthiest world economy is attained when trade is at its freest. This should be our goal.

Aid to Less Developed Nations

Our principles and ideals impel us to aid the new nations.

13. THE DEFENSE OF THE FREE WORLD

14. DISARMAMENT

Since a major nuclear war would be a world catastophe, the limitation and control of nuclear armament is imperative. Disarmament should be our ultimate goal. It cannot be attained without eliminating the sources of distrust and fear among nations. Hence, our immediate task must be the step-by-step advance toward control of nuclear weapons and their means of delivery, with effective international inspection. A safeguarded agreement to suspend nuclear testing may well be the first step and would tend to limit the number of nuclear powers.

In view of the complex interaction of arms control and national security, we must organize a major government effort for the study and analysis of political, military, and technical issues in order to provide a sounder basis for policy formulation and negotiation.

15. THE UNITED NATIONS

A key goal in the pursuit of a vigorous and effective United States foreign policy is the preservation and strengthening of the United Nations. Over the next decade, it will be under tremendous strain. However, it remains the chief instrument available for building a genuine community of nations.

A CONCLUDING WORD

The very deepest goals for Americans relate to the spiritual health of our people. The right of every individual to seek God and the well-springs of truth, each in his own way, is infinitely precious. We must continue to guarantee it, and we must exercise it, for ours is a spiritually-based society. Our material achievements in fact represent a triumph of the spirit of man in the mastery of his material environment.

The family is at the heart of society. The educational process begins and is served most deeply in the home.

The American citizen in the years ahead ought to devote a larger portion of his time and energy directly to the solution of the nation's problems.

Above all, Americans must demonstrate in every aspect of their lives the fallacy of a purely selfish attitude—the materialistic ethic. Indifference to poverty and disease is inexcusable in a society dedicated to the dignity of the individual; so also is indifference to values other than material comfort and national power. Our faith is that man lives, not by bread alone, but by self-respect, by regard for other men, by convictions of right and wrong, by strong religious faith.

Man has never been an island unto himself. The shores of his concern have expanded from his neighborhood to his nation, and from his nation to his world. Free men have always known the necessity for responsibility. A basic goal for each American is to achieve a sense of responsibility as broad as his world-wide concerns and as compelling as the dangers and opportunities he confronts.

CHAPTER SEVEN

The Principle
of Public Responsibility

The Central Theme
The Limits of Involvement
Public Policy, Corporate Morality, and Law
Public Responsibility

We are now ready to draw together the main elements of our analysis and to present a summary statement of our central theme and its implications. This recapitulation integrates the analysis in the previous chapters and provides a framework for the discussion of implementation techniques in those following.

THE CENTRAL THEME

In the mainstream of liberal economic and social analysis, the nature of the private firm and its relationship with the larger society have been analyzed in terms of the market contract model, an analytical conception that underlies the traditional "fundamentalist" doctrine of managerial responsibility. However, a gradual process of social change—stimulated by continuing intellectual and political criticism, the increasing prominence and influence of large corporations in society, and many other factors—has led to a general weakening of the fundamentalist position and to an increased awareness of managerial social involvement. This changed orientation has lacked a coherent rationale, but has resulted in a diverse array of corporate policies and practices justified in terms of a vague and somewhat moralistic doctrine of "social responsibility."

Increased awareness of social involvement is simply a recognition of reality. And the reality of management-society relationships can be described in terms of interpenetrating systems, not in terms of market contract. Managerial involvement in the larger society is a natural phenomenon, giving rise to multiple contacts and considerations. And, similarly, the involvement of the larger society in organizational management is normal, varied, and continuing.

Over the whole range of social involvement—which, for analytical purposes, we break down into primary and secondary areas—both the firm and the larger society require mechanisms for communication, adaptation, and mutual influence. For some activities and impacts, the transactions mechanism of the market is sufficient; for others, however, the market mechanism is inadequate or nonexistent. The general and underlying mechanism for mutual interpenetration between the managerial unit and its host environment is the public policy process, which provides both a framework for, and a supplement to, the operation of firms and markets.

Building upon this analysis, we propose the principle of public responsibility as a thesis or guideline. This principle is, in relation to the interpenetrating systems model and our analysis of the public policy process, exactly analogous to the fundamentalist doctrine in relation to the market contract model. According to this principle, the scope of managerial responsibility is not unlimited, as the popular conception of "social responsibility" might suggest, but specifically defined in terms of primary and secondary involvement areas. Within the defined scope, the goals of managerial activity, their relative priority, and the criteria for appraising success and failure are defined both by the market mechanism and by public policy.

THE LIMITS OF INVOLVEMENT

Our analysis of the scope of managerial responsibility begins with the concept of *primary involvement*. The area of primary involvement is determined by the specialized functional role of the organization, the role that defines its nature and social purpose and that provides the basis for exchange relationships between it and the rest of society. Viable primary involvement relationships, tested and mediated through the market mechanism, are essential to the existence of the organization over time. If a firm cannot maintain a symbiotic relationship with the rest of society, fulfilling a "social purpose," it will become an object of charity or cease to exist. Of course, management can add and drop specialized activities and re-orient primary involvement contacts in order to maintain the organization. And, correspondingly, society can alter its own relationships with individual firms in order to assure their continuation through time (changing tax rates or granting subsidies to avoid business failures and plant closings, for example). In any event, managerial responsibility begins with the primary involvement area.

The area of *secondary involvement* includes all those relationships, activities, and impacts of the organization that are ancillary or consequential to its primary involvement activities. Secondary involvement impacts include the *use* (by others) of merchandise and services sold, the consequences of production and sales activities themselves, the impact of procurement and employment, the neighborhood effects of physical plant occupancy, and so on.

For a more detailed example of primary and secondary involvement, consider one of the major producers of automobiles. The actual production process, marketing and advertising, procurement of components and inputs, employment and wages are all part of the primary involvement activity of the firm. Even the most traditional view of the social role of the firm would find these activities within its scope of responsibility (whatever criteria might be applied in dealing with them). The concept of secondary involvement expands the scope of managerial responsibility quite considerably, although mostly to areas that have already been brought to managerial attention on an *ad hoc* or crisis basis. With respect to product *use,* such secondary involvement issues include, for example, safety, environmental pollution, and the land-use implications of an expanding road-highway network. Employment-related issues include the human impact of assembly-line work, training opportunities for disadvantaged workers, and hours and overtime requirements. Other issues involve relationships with dealers and suppliers, impact of production facilities on their physical environments (pollution, congestion, visual acceptability), and so forth. [1]

We avoid here a metaphor of "concentric circles," or a distinction between "economic products" and "social products"—phrases used to describe the expanded purview of micro-unit management in the classic work of Bowen. [2] Secondary involvement may extend very far in some directions— say, to the final use of consumer goods, including both safety and life-style aspects—and only a limited distance in others; the ranges of impact are not concentric. Further, the "economic" aspect of a secondary involvement issue—say, pension benefits—may be its principal feature, and additional "social" implications derivative therefrom. Thus, we feel that the concept of secondary involvement, which implies the pursuit of effects and implications to *their* ends, whether nearby or remote, economic or social, provides a more useful terminology and approach.

The areas of primary and secondary involvement combined, then, serve to define the scope of organizational interpenetration with society and to separate the sphere of managerial responsibility from the whole of social life. Some such separation or limitation is necessary if any guideline for corporate

[1] Although the paragraph above was written quite independently, it is notable that General Motors Corporation's *1973 Report on Progress in Areas of Public Concern* (GM Technical Center, Warren, Michigan; February 8, 1973) contains chapters on each of the listed topics.

[2] Howard R. Bowen, *Social Responsibilities of the Businessman* (New York: Harper & Brothers, 1953).

social performance is to be implemented and evaluated; and the absence of limitations has been a principal and valid fundamentalist criticism of popular versions of the "social responsibility" doctrine. To repeat, managerial responsibility, in our view, extends as far as the limits of secondary involvement, *but no farther.* It is not the case, as some "social responsibility" enthusiasts apparently hold, that the private firm is charged with improving social conditions or resolving social problems regardless of their character or cause. Discharge of such a range of responsibilities would constitute an impossible task; more important, the concept of an unlimited sphere of obligations offers no guidance as to the directions or goals that should be pursued in the limited activities that might, in fact, be undertaken.

To further emphasize the importance of boundaries, return to the example of the automobile manufacturing company. Important general social concerns lying clearly *outside* its primary and secondary involvement areas—and therefore *not* within the scope of managerial responsibility—are the public education system, environmental issues unrelated to the automobile (water quality, for example), housing standards and availability, general public health and medical insurance programs, and political process issues, such as voting rights. Thus, although the list of secondary involvement areas for a large and powerful firm in this large and important industry is, indeed, very comprehensive, it does not include all—or even *most*—of the major concerns and problems of society as a whole.

There may be need for a further word concerning the connection between social involvement and the tactic of responding to protests and complaints by various "publics." Autonomous and often surprising objections and demands have frequently been the first evidence received by corporate managers that some other elements within society were not totally satisfied with their performance. One conventional initial response has been to question the "legitimacy" of such views; a more modern response is to recognize any and all such reflections of social dissatisfaction as "our problem, whether we like it or not." In a sense, the latter response is realistic and essentially correct. However, it is subject to two serious pitfalls. One is the tendency to define the scope of involvement *only* in terms of the complaints of those elements of society that have been heard from; that is, to take managerial cognizance only of negative views brought forward by others. The second pitfall is the view that any and all such expressions of opinion are equally valid and deserving of attention. The concept of primary and secondary involvement corrects both of these errors. In the first place, the sphere of managerial involvement is defined, whether or not persons and entities within its scope are well-satisfied, and whether or not they voluntarily express their views. Further, this more limited concept makes it possible to examine the legitimacy and priority of demands and complaints against an objective frame of reference, rather than simply in terms of subjective criteria and traditional practices.

Any area of social life excluded from managerial concern as a result of this analysis might, of course, come to be included as a result of changing circumstances. The notion of a boundary between organizational involvement areas and the "rest of the world" is general; the boundary is to be breached and shifted over time. Further, any individual manager may, *as a private citizen,* become concerned or involved in any area of social life and adjust his personal schedule and role accordingly. The concept of secondary involvement limits the purview of management as *management*—that is, as persons vested with responsibility and authority within organizations—but does not limit in any way the personal values or activities of individuals. On the contrary, the primary and secondary involvement concepts permit the reestablishment of a distinction between organizational and personal goals and motives, a distinction that is absolutely necessary if long-term *organizational* commitment to societal goals and processes is to be made.

In sum, if organizational management is to become responsible for its social impact and performance in areas not adequately mediated by the market mechanism and reflected in established financial accounting and reporting procedures, the *scope* of such responsibility will prove satisfactory in an environment of dynamic change. Hence, a viable guideline for social involvement requires a criterion for determining the *scope* for managerial responsibility, a basis for answering the question: *Is this really our affair?* The question can be definitely answered by reference to the concepts of primary and secondary involvement and by tracing out the impact of organizational activity to see whether or not it touches any specific area of social life in any particular way.

PUBLIC POLICY, CORPORATE MORALITY, AND LAW

If the scope of managerial responsibility extends to, but not beyond, the limits of the primary and secondary involvement of its respective organization in the larger society, what goals are to be pursued, what standards of performance applied, to managerial performance? It is impossible to test this broad range of relationships against the fundamentalist criterion of profitability. Hence, it is necessary to search elsewhere for goals and criteria; to ask the question: How are responsible managers to know good from bad, better from worse, success from failure, with respect to their social performance?

This question is more difficult to answer than it may sound, and it is not made easier by the fact that the great bulk of the "social responsibility" literature *assumes* that the answer is obvious. Consider, for example, the issue of employment opportunities for minority or disadvantaged workers. The management of any organization operating in a location in which such potential employees are available may consider this issue appropriate for its consideration. But what is the goal to be sought, the criterion on success? The easy answer is "more"—i.e., more employment opportunities. Yet hasty acceptance of "more" as an answer dodges all the important questions. How do you know that "more" is the answer? And does a response to "more" imply discharging existing employees, making new jobs available, creating training or internship programs, providing auxiliary employee services (transportation, day-care, and so on), advertising job opportunities in appropriate media, or simply adding qualified applicants to the potential employment lists if they appear voluntarily?

To find the answers to these questions of emphasis and implementation, we have to go back to the source of the "more" answer itself—public policy. Increased employment opportunities for minority and disadvantaged workers is an appropriate goal and guideline for managerial responsibility because the social decision-making system of our society has made it so. Evolving from informal, essentially moralistic, and not widely accepted efforts to prevent physical abuse and economic subjugation, the current goal of expanded work and career opportunities is reflected in a variety of explicit public policy measures and, more generally, in the atmosphere and attitude that permits such measures to be adopted and that is, in turn, promoted by them. Hence, in our own society at the present time, promoting employment opportunities for minority and disadvantaged workers is specifically within the scope of managerial responsibility. At the same time, it is *not* public policy that current employees be discharged in order to permit the creation of such jobs, or that minority and disadvantaged workers be simply hired for jobs that they cannot perform and then either kept on as "charity" or released for poor performance. On the contrary, high turnover of minority employees and mere "window-dressing" appointments are not generally regarded as contributing at all to social performance goals.

Public policy differs from general good behavior and moralistic guidelines, just as it differs from the specific and literal content of statute law. Although there is plenty of room for disagreement, both with respect to the policy agenda and with respect to the substance of specific policy measures, there can be no thought that public policy is something about which each individual can have his own unique vision, that its character varies—like most ethical and moral judgments—from person to person and case to case. Nor is public policy limited to those situations in which society is willing to use compulsion and the judicial mechanism to achieve its objectives.

We specifically reject Andrews' proposal that "the best corporations be made moral" by their acceptance of a concept of "social responsibility" that includes voluntary charitable contributions, "an ethical level of operations," choices based on "imputed social worth," and "investment for reasons other than . . . economic return."[3] Personalistic guidelines such as these suggest

---

[3] Kenneth R. Andrews, "Can the Best Corporations Be Made Moral?" *Harvard Business Review*, May-June, 1973. An affirmative answer to Andrews' question is suggested by Raymond

that the whole matter, like whether or not to have flowers in the office, is one of taste. As Chamberlain emphasizes, "There is a profound difference between the ethical standard governing personal conduct and the organizational imperative governing insitutional conduct."[4] The resort to personal ethical standards seems to eliminate all operational content from the analysis of managerial involvement in society; certainly, it provides more basis for disagreement than for agreement.

An appropriately broad orientation toward the complex of standards, norms, and expectations involved in the relationship between corporate management and other elements of society, individually and collectively, is suggested by the term "the rules of the game," frequently employed by Friedman, Chamberlain, and other critics of popular notions of "social responsibility." The "rules" of the socio-economic game being played by private business units in our society are nowhere comprehensively stated. On the contrary, they are reflected in a great variety of statues and programs and, more importantly, in the underlying context of general economic and social traditions and values. Corporate management is concerned not only with the current content of the rules—what activities are involved and what performance is required or prohibited—but also with the directions in which the rules are changing and the processes by which such changes are brought about. Indeed, like a constitutional provision providing for amendment, a procedure for changing the rules is an essential part of the rules themselves. (Societies in which the rules of the game can be changed only by revolutions *have* revolutions.)

The "rules of the game," as reflected and modified within the broad framework of public policy, provide a guide for managerial behavior more objective than individual moral or ethical insights and more general than the literal text of statutes and regulations. Public policy includes the spirit of the law as well as the letter. Further, *policy* exists even in areas of social life in which there is no specific *letter* of law for reference. Clearly, there are many areas of social concern in which formal statutory requirements, judicial interpretation, and executive enforcement are expensive, largely ineffective, and perhaps even repugnant. It does not, however, follow that these areas are excluded from the reach of public policy or from the scope of managerial responsibility.

Public policy is not only different from individual moral judgments and personal concepts of "what's good for people"; it is also different from the specific goals and interests of narrowly defined interest groups and special publics. Hence, emphasis on public policy as a source of managerial

---

Baumhart, *Ethics in Business* (New York: Holt, Rinehart and Winston, 1968). By contrast, a negative answer is strongly indicated by the personal experiences recorded in Robert L. Heilbroner *et al., In the Name of Profit* (Garden City, N.Y.: Doubleday, 1972).

[4] Neil W. Chamberlain, *The Limits of Corporate Responsibility* (New York: Basic Books, Inc., Publishers, 1973), p. 205. A similar view is expressed by Max Ways, "Business Faces Growing Pressures," *Fortune,* May, 1974, pp. 193ff.

guidelines and appraisal criteria contrasts sharply with superficially similar suggestions based on an "interest group" analysis. One recent proposal contends, for example, that "the best strategy for the corporation is to develop a systematic mechanism by which to measure the preferences of various groups for corporate actions and the relative strengths of these groups to affect corporate welfare."[5]   Although we would agree that opinion monitoring is an important element in an ongoing program of environmental scanning, we doubt that corporate social involvement and impact can be accurately appraised through an "interest group" approach.

The various ways by which issues are brought onto the public policy agenda and specific policies themselves are formulated and revised over time have been discussed in preceding chapters. Public policy is dynamic because it reflects a dynamic environment and therefore provides an appropriate guide for individual and organizational activity within that environment. At the same time, public policy exists on many levels—from widely understood and accepted standards, through specific laws and requirements, including newly emerging viewpoints and issues. There may be a certain ambiguity, or even conflict, with regard to equally substantial public policy guidelines and directives. And, hence, there may be honest differences of opinion as to the particular guideline or criterion to be applied in some specific situation. On the other hand, ambiguity and variety within the policy framework permit a considerable amount of individual variation and experimentation. Hence, it is not inconsistent to say that public policy in many areas includes the principle of adaptation and modification in individual cases, within a broad guideline as to the desired direction of change or character of performance.

To repeat, the recognition of public policy as a source of goals, criteria, and priorities for micro-unit management is *not* simply an emphasis on formal statute law, and is still less a demand for increased government regulation. On the contrary, as Andrews earlier emphasized, "to argue that businessman should knowingly ignore the consequences of his company's impact upon its physical and social environment until new laws are passed is in this day wantonly irresponsibile in itself."[6]   The point is that the public policy process is, in our society, the means by which society as a whole articulates its goals and objectives, and directs and stimulates individuals and

[5] Allan D. Shocker and S. Prakash Sethi, "An Approach to Incorporating Societal Preferences in Developing Corporate Action Strategies," *California Management Review,* XV, No. 4 (1973), p. 99. See also, M. Dierkes and Robert Coppock, "Corporate Responsibility Does Not Depend on Public Pressure," *Business and Society Review,* No. 6 (Summer 1973), pp. 82-89.

[6] Kenneth Andrews, "Public Responsibility in the Private Corporation," *The Journal of Industrial Economics,* XX, No. 2 (1972), p. 139. The general viewpoint of Andrews and his associates, apart from their special "moral" emphasis, is very closely akin to our own. See C. Roland Christensen, Kenneth R. Andrews and Joseph L. Bower, "The Company and Its Societal Responsibilities," *Business Policy* (Homewood, Ill.: Richard D. Irwin, Inc., 1973), pp. 578-85; and K.R. Andrews, *The Concept of Corporate Strategy* (Homewood, Ill.: Dow-Jones Irwin, 1971), Chap. 5, "The Company and Its Social Responsibilities: Relating Corporate Strategy to the Needs of Society."

organizations to contribute to and cooperate with them. Hence, appropriate guidelines for managerial performance are to be found not in the personal visions of the managers themselves or in the special interests of any particular pressure group or constituency, but rather in the larger society. And the social process of policy formation is, as previously noted, continuous and evolutionary; the goals and standards of yesterday are modified for today and will be altered again tomorrow.

PUBLIC RESPONSIBILITY

We have chosen the term *public responsibility* to describe our particular thesis from among several alternatives. Although subject to some confusion with "social responsibility," the term preserves the desirable notion that management is responsible—i.e., "likely to be called upon to answer . . . as to the primary cause, motive or agent, . . . creditable or chargeable with the result . . .; liable or subject to legal review; . . . politically answerable. . . ."[7] —for the impact of its activities, whether intended or not. As the fundamentalist critics have emphasized, a strict interpretation of responsibility is necessary for any serious consideration of implementation and appraisal. We choose the word *public* rather than *social*, of course, in order to stress the importance of the public policy process, rather than individual opinion and conscience, as the source of goals and appraisal criteria.

Any broadening of the scope of managerial responsibility raises the problem of balancing multiple objectives, but this problem is neither new, nor peculiar to issues of social involvement. Corporate management is routinely responsible, for example, for money, plant, employee safety, and product quality. The notion that "it all comes down to profit" is nonsense, if the reported "profit" results from over-commitment of working capital to inventory and sales promotion, deterioration of facilities due to neglected maintenance, inadequate safety protection followed by accidents, fines and lawsuits, or one-time sales made to unsuspecting purchasers of defective merchandise. All of these tactics can be converted into "profit" in some accounting report; but they are rarely associated with competent or successful management over the long term.

Furthermore, corporate management is almost invariably concerned with *both* profitability indicators *and* volume or market share goals. Additional volume and market share can often be "bought" at some sacrifice of profitability; and, conversely, a slight reduction in market share and sales goals can often generate a short-run increase in profits (due to dropping high-cost services and customers, for example). Management routinely balances these and other competing or noncomparable objectives—includ-

[7] *Webster's Third New International Dictionary,* unabridged (Springfield, Mass.: G. & C. Merriam Company, Publishers, 1971), p. 1935.

ing, particularly, the achievement of different performance levels over different time periods and the maintenance of an organizational environment that is at once harmonious and strongly motivating. Hence, the notion that managers cannot be held responsible for performance in terms of multiple objectives or that "it all comes down to profit" in any strict sense is a naive oversimplification and always has been.

More important than any conflict with a single-minded emphasis on profitability, the broad range of qualitative issues raised for managerial consideration by the principle of public responsibility appears to conflict sharply with a conspicuous intellectual trend of the past quarter century: the development of management science. At the most elementary level, management science simply involves an emphasis on observation, measurement, formal modeling, and hypothesis testing. Following this trend, analytical work in accounting, marketing, finance, and other functional areas of management has come to "look like" analytical work in physics, chemistry, or biology. This superficial similarity, reflecting a common reliance on mathematical and statistical techniques and on the analysis of numerical data, has contributed to the popularity of the notion that management could *be* like physics, in the sense that precise and reproducible answers could be provided in response to rigorously stated analytical questions.

A more generous characterization of both management and science, and therefore of management science, may be framed in terms of a learning process under conditions of ignorance and uncertainty, including uncertainty about the goals that managerial activity is supposed to pursue. When the concept of management science is broadened to include the process of value determination and learning, the apparent conflict between the precise optimization solutions provided by the scientific manager and the broader social issues raised through public policy is substantially reduced, if not eliminated. The possibility then arises that social, ethical and moral issues might be drawn into the framework of management science itself. This latter possibility has been particularly stressed in the work of C. W. Churchman, who argues specifically that value issues cannot be eliminated from managerial analysis because of their alleged "unscientific" character.[8]

Even to a sympathetic reader, it may appear that the public responsibility approach, like the other "social involvement" views previously discussed, involves service to two masters—the market on one side and the vague requests of "society" on the other. If so, our view could simply be another version of a "profit-plus" philosophy. However, we argue that this is not the case. Some of the things that the managerial unit can do for society can be stimulated, discouraged, or directed through the market mechanism; others cannot. Assignment of particular functions to market control on one hand and to policy control on the other is itself a public policy decision of the first

[8] C. West Churchman, *Prediction and Optimal Decision* (Englewood Cliffs, N.J.: Prentice-Hall, Inc., 1961).

magnitude. Therefore, operation of the market exchange mechanism is itself within the framework of public policy and can be modified or eliminated correspondingly. Thus, there is really only one master for the corporation—society at large.

Thoughtful spokesmen for the business community have repeatedly acknowledged that this is the case. As the CED statement put it: "Business functions by public consent, and its basic purpose is to serve constructively the needs of society—to the satisfaction of society."[9] Similarly, the Confederation of British Industry declared: "The public limited company is an artificial creation of law that owes its existence to the will of the community. . . . Companies do not exist by right but will continue only so long as society finds them useful."[10]

Our conception of *public responsibility* not only answers the two essential questions of scope and criteria that must be dealt with in any serious approach to the problem of corporate social involvement, but it is also a particularly appropriate response to the overwhelmingly important characteristic of the world in which we live—rapid and pervasive change of every kind. The attempt to define either the scope or, still more, the character of managerial responsibility in terms of specific rules—production and marketing, for scope; "be a good citizen" and "do what is right," for criteria—can be taken seriously only within a stable environmental context. *If* the larger social environment were in fact stable, then we might indeed be able to define particular roles and responsibilities for individual organizations and expect them to be valid guidelines year in and year out. But our environment is conspicuously unstable, and therefore our guidelines and appraisal criteria have to be stated in terms of the *process* by which they are determined and changed, not in terms of specific rules, standards, or goals. Hence, recognition of the public policy process as the source of guidelines and standards for managerial responsibility serves to resolve the problem of goals and criteria more clearly than a specific—and soon outdated—list of "do's and don'ts." In our rapidly changing environment, any such specific set of topics and guidelines would become quickly obsolete. The process by which problems are identified and guidelines developed is, however, central and continuing.

Our viewpoint is very closely akin to that summarized by Eli Goldston in the following five propositions:[11]

[9] Committee for Economic Development, *Social Responsibilities of Business Corporations* (New York: Committee for Economic Development, 1971), p. 11.

[10] Company Affairs Committee, *The Responsibilities of the British Public Company* (London: Confederation of British Industry; final report, endorsed by the CBI Council on September 19, 1973), p. 8.

[11] Eli Goldston, *The Quantification of Concern* (Pittsburgh: Carnegie-Mellon University, 1971), p. 60.

(1) The selection of goals and priorities is a public political decision. The business manager participates as just another voting citizen and argues his specific interests as just another affected party.

(2) Government budgets, particularly the Federal budget, are the principal expression of our goals and priorities.

(3) The private firm responds to the carrot of profit and the whip of cost, but exhortation of managers can be effective within a limited range.

(4) As our values change, we need new measures of national and of corporate performance.

(5) The performance reports must be reviewed by outside auditors, but some matters are beyond quantification and can be checked only by field inspection.

Each of Goldston's propositions echoes and summarizes theses developed in our own analysis. The last two points identify the tasks ahead—implementation decisions and performance measurement, and the accountability of management to itself and to the public at large.

CHAPTER EIGHT

Implementation: Scanning and Process Responses

Scanning the Social Environment
Informal Scanning
Formal Scanning: Two Approaches
Activity-based Scanning
Societal Scanning
Delphi Technique
Other Baseline Projections
Surveys and Opinion Research
Internal Scanning

Process Responses to Social Involvement
Cognizance
Reporting
Participation
Experimentation

Summary

Suppose that the management of an organization has experienced the socialization process described in Chapter 4 and has accepted the principle of public responsibility as a basis for defining its sphere of responsibility and performance goals. It now faces the task of implementing this decision, both with respect to the *process* by which managerial plans are formulated and operations carried out and with respect to the *substance* of specific decisions and actions.

Three essential elements are involved. First, the organization requires a means of defining its own areas of involvement in specific terms and identifying the public policy considerations, trends, and objectives relevant to its spheres of activity. This requirement can be met through the process of *scanning*. The second requirement is a set of techniques or procedures that can be used to make and carry out decisions resulting from this new perspective. Many of these techniques involve the *process* of management—taking informal cognizance of societal issues, formal reporting, encouraging participation of diverse interests in management decisions, and experimentation. The scanning process itself and these process-oriented implementation techniques are discussed in this chapter. Other aspects of implementation involve specific policy actions and structural change, and these are discussed in Chapter 9. The third required element in the implementation process, the development of techniques for evaluation and control, is still in a primitive state. However, progress is being made, and a number of examples can be presented. Since most of these techniques involve the evaluation of structural changes and substantive decisions, rather than process responses to socialization, they are discussed in the latter half of Chapter 9, after the survey of other implementation practices has been completed.

Throughout this discussion of implementation, we have cited examples of actual activity wherever possible. Our selection of examples does not, of course, imply that the individuals and groups involved are in agreement with, or have even heard of, our own particular point of view. On the contrary, we have simply chosen examples—however initiated and motivated—that appear consistent with the public responsibility thesis or that illustrate techniques that might be used to implement it.

SCANNING THE SOCIAL ENVIRONMENT

Scanning is the selective and systematic gathering, synthesis, and analysis of information. The scanning process is basic to the implementation of the principle of public responsibility since it is through scanning that the microorganization identifies the extent of its involvement in society, discovers relevant social issues and public policy goals, and develops ideas for implementation techniques and responses. Scanning can be formal or informal, simple or complex; and scanning, like any other activity, is subject to appraisal in cost-benefit terms. We argue that systematic and continuous environmental scanning within a comprehensive framework is an essential activity for any ongoing managerial organization of any size, comparable to annual budget preparation and review or the preparation of regular operating statements.[1]

[1] Francis J. Aguilar, *Scanning the Business Environment* (New York: The Macmillan Company, 1967), is the only comprehensive study of organizational scanning. The work concentrates on the process of scanning for the sole purpose of strategic planning in primary involvement areas. On a more theoretical level, see Amitai Etzioni, *The Active Society* (New York: The Free Press, 1968), Chap. 7, pp. 282-309.

Informal Scanning

Mere existence within a social setting generates an information base and sources of routine data and stimuli that constitute an informal scanning system. The variety of sources that may be involved is well summarized by Aguilar's list (see Exhibit 8-1). These varied sources are available to every

EXHIBIT 8-1

Sources of Organizational Information

Outside Sources

Personal Sources

Outside members
- - Customers
- - Suppliers
- - Others (e.g., bankers, consultants, persons in associated companies such as a licensee)

Nonmembers
- - Outside business and professional associates
- - Others (e.g., chance encounters, neighbors)

Impersonal Sources

Publications
- - Trade publications
- - Newspapers

All other impersonal sources (e.g., technical conference, trade show, exhibition, schedule report from a consultant, visual or other direct perception of an event or condition)

Inside Sources

Personal Sources

Subordinates

Peers

Superiors

Others

Impersonal Sources

Regular and general reports and notices (e.g., salesman's call report, R&D department's monthly progress report)

Scheduled meetings

Source: Francis J. Aguilar, *Scanning the Business Environment* (New York: The Macmillan Company, 1967), p. 66.

manager and are the particular concerns of individuals assigned the specific task of "knowing what's going on." The number and variety of information sources, however, gives rise to two problems. One is that the scanning of these sources, particularly on an informal basis, cannot hope to be complete, simply because they are too numerous. The second is that information from various sources is distorted, incomplete, overlapping and contradictory; hence, synthesis and evaluation is required even when the initial information-gathering process is left largely to routine and chance contacts.

Although informal scanning is to some extent inevitable and certainly better than none at all, Aguilar emphasizes its many inadequacies. He found numerous examples in which a particular bit of information—collected at the outset by chance contact rather than systematic search—was given dissimilar meanings by different managers. For example, chance bits of knowledge gained about a newly opened local business, a competitor's backward integration, or another firm's intentions to enter the export market were interpreted differently—in both content and importance—by different members of the same organization. Information concerning changing social trends and public issues is obviously subject to even greater variability in selective perception, interpretation, and appraisal.

In actual practice, informal scanning involves a combination of general awareness, evaluation through experience and judgment, and hoped-for serendipity (the ability to discover valuable things by chance). In an increasingly complex environment, however, informal scanning provides an inadequate information base for management decisions.

Formal Scanning: Two Approaches

Formal scanning is intended to reduce—although it cannot eliminate—problems of selective perception, distortion, and incompleteness of information and to provide a basis for synthesis and evaluation over time. A baseline of factual knowledge in relevant information areas is created, and systematic procedures are followed to fill in gaps and maintain currency. Although general scanning functions can be widely dispersed throughout an organization—and responsibility for scanning relevant to specific operating areas will often be assigned to managers within those areas themselves—general environmental scanning and synthesis of information must occur at the top organizational staff level. Only in this way can the results of the scanning process become an integral part of top-level managerial decision making and long-range planning.

The appropriate format for environmental scanning depends in part upon a particular management's view of its own functions and of the role of its organization within society. If the organization's current areas of specialization are the principal concerns of management, the scanning mechanism may be based on an *activity approach* in which each primary involvement activity is traced out to reveal its secondary aspects and impact. By contrast, an organization contemplating major changes in its primary involvement areas, or one so highly diversified that an endless list of individual activities would be involved, may adopt a *societal overview approach.* In this case, the scanning process is structured around the major areas of concern or change within the larger society, and their implications are traced backward to discover their specific impact, if any, on the managerial unit. Each of these polar approaches to environmental scanning has its own strengths and weaknesses, and a combination of both approaches can be adopted. Nevertheless, somewhat different formats and techniques appear to be useful for each of them, and they merit separate discussion.

Activity-Based Scanning

The assumption underlying the activity approach to scanning is that the basic challenges and issues facing the corporation will develop from sources already within its operating environment. Thus, the first scanning task is to develop a map or model of the present environment, beginning with the area of primary involvement and extending into secondary areas in all relevant directions. This "mapping" of the terrain will reveal instances of pressure and conflict, as well as of harmony or synergy, and thus generate a concrete agenda of issues and problems requiring managerial consideration.

A simple framework for activity-based scanning is illustrated in Exhibit 8-2. We assume that the organization involved is engaged in three broad types of activity: operations (production and distribution), management of human resources (all personnel-related matters), and communications (advertising, public relations, customer and supplier contact). Further, we assume that the organization's management sees itself as involved in three sets of basic relationships: those mediated directly through the marketplace; those involving specific governmental units and agencies; and those involving the community and society at large.

Within the three-by-three matrix of Exhibit 8-2, the implications of each of the organization's main types of activity for each level of environmental contact can be traced out. The initial analysis will be descriptive and rather obvious. Nevertheless, as additional points are noted—and subordinate rows and columns added—similar terms will begin to appear, and inconsistencies and problem areas will be identified. In some cases the same words (e.g., "consumerism," "minority groups," "pollution") will appear in different connections, and hence a major area of external concern will be discovered. In other instances, obvious inconsistencies—"high product quality"/"low wages," "plant is eyesore"/"good community relations"—will appear. In the end, the organization will have ascertained one or more areas of involvement that should become subject to continued managerial concern.

Many recent examples of corporate social reporting are based on an activity-scanning approach, and the general validity of this approach has

EXHIBIT 8-2

Activity Approach Matrix for Environmental Scanning

	Market Contacts	Government Units and Agencies	Community and Society
Operations	Price; Quality; Distribution policy	Consumer legislation; Price control	Consumerism movement
Human Resources	Wage levels and rates; Employment structure	Discrimination; Equal employment opportunity	Population and labor force participation; Local economy
Communications	Advertising; Disclosure of information	Lobbying; Reporting requirements	Publicity; Response to community inquiries; Participation in local affairs

been formally argued by Sethi, among others.[2] An early and influential example was Eli Goldston's statement, "Toward Social Accounting," published as an insert into the annual report of Eastern Gas and Fuel Associates, 1972.[3] Goldston's statement deals with only four topics: industrial safety, minority employment, charitable giving, and pensions. He notes that:

> The topics for this first report were not chosen because they are necessarily the most important ones, or the ones that might make us look good, but because they are the most readily measurable, because our goals with respect to them are comparatively simple and clear, and because they lie in areas where management can rather directly influence results. In addition, managerial decisions on these topics can have a significant impact on earnings per share.

As a result of the scanning and reporting activity in these four areas, he concluded:

> Our industrial accident record in recent years has not been very good. . . . [But with respect to] the severity rate, which takes into account time lost as a result of accidents . . . , Eastern's record has been steadier, and apparently more in line with other firms for our industries.

[2] S. Prakash Sethi, "Getting a Handle on the Social Audit," *Business and Society Review* (Winter 1972-73), pp. 31-38; and "Corporate Social Audit: An Emerging Trend in Measuring Corporate Social Performance," in *The Corporate Dilemma,* ed. Dow Votaw and S. Prakash Sethi (Englewood Cliffs, N.J.: Prentice-Hall, Inc., 1973), pp. 214-31.

[3] Eli Goldston, "Toward Social Accounting," *Annual Report* (Eastern Gas and Fuel Associates, 1972, insert).

• • •

It is difficult to generalize fairly and judiciously about Eastern's minority employment statistics. Numerically, minority employment in the company has increased in recent years, but has not quite maintained its percentage proportion. . . . Boston Gas has had an excellent record of integrating its work force, but the addition of new territory with a different population mix has appeared to slow the trend.

• • •

The Federal Income Tax law permits contributions to the extent of 5% of taxable income; many studies, however, have shown that the majority of large public corporations make charitable gifts of about 1% of pre-tax income. We have been using this 1% figure as a guide so far as Foundation gifts are concerned.

• • •

Eastern's employees participate in one of the 23 separate formal retirement plans to which the company and its subsidiaries are a party. . . . Eighteen of the formal retirement plans are maintained by negotiations in collective bargaining with various labor unions. . . . We believe that the expense, the benefits and vesting provisions of our numerous retirement plans are reasonably in line with those of the different industries in which we operate.

Societal Scanning

The societal overview approach to scanning essentially involves an opposite process. Instead of beginning with the current activities of the organization and following them outward to discover their impact, one begins with an assessment of current trends and concerns within society as a whole and then attempts to deduce their implications for the organization. The basic assumption underlying this approach is that the organization itself is subject to considerable change in the light of broad social developments; hence, these developments—rather than current primary activities—provide the basic framework of analysis.

An immediate question arises as to how the major concerns and trends of society are to be identified. Several examples of techniques currently being used for this purpose may be briefly mentioned.

Delphi Technique

Among the more popular methods of forecasting and assessing trends is the Delphi technique, a method based on "group estimation" procedures. The rationale for the Delphi technique is that no one has certain knowledge of the future, and individual speculation is of little value; nevertheless, individuals hold opinions that are based upon some evidence and experience, constituting an "informed judgment." The Delphi method involves securing the informed judgment of recognized experts in diverse fields. Through the use of anonymous projections, re-evaluation, and controlled feedback, a composite statistical picture of group response is obtained. One description states: "The net result of a Delphi exercise is a convergence toward a common group estimate. . . . It is opinion that has been moved from a lower to a higher level of probable validity."[4] The Delphi technique is useful for identifying the principal dimensions of change and types of forces to be involved in an environmental scanning analysis, as well as a source of specific predictions and trends.

Variants of the Delphi technique are frequently employed by "futurist"-oriented research groups, such as the Institute for the Future, Hudson Institute, and the Futures Group.[5] In the late 1960s, the General Electric Company conducted its own Delphi study of major trends in the business environment.[6] Utilizing a panel composed of educators, government, press, and trade association representatives, the G.E. study culminated in the identification of eight trends likely to have major social implications before 1980: increasing affluence, economic stabilization, a rising tide of education, changing attitudes toward work and leisure, growing interdependence of institutions, emergence of the "post-industrial" society, strengthening of pluralism and individualism, and a complex of matters identified as the "Negro/Urban Problem." After obtaining some expert consensus on the nature and genuineness of these trends, it then remained for G.E. management to analyze the special significance of these trends for the company.

Other Baseline Projections

The costliness of the Delphi approach gives rise to a need for alternative methods of generating baseline projections. One of the more common alternatives is a projection based on expert views as reflected in current literature. The major trade association in the life insurance industry (The Institute of Life Insurance) has, for example, developed a methodological process by which personnel from member firms appraise specific categories of current literature in widely diverse fields. By identifying significant articles and bringing them to the attention of the association's research staff, member firm personnel act as monitors of experts' perceptions of the future. The association's research staff analyzes the information brought to its attention, synthesizes it, and develops a series of periodic "trend analysis projections." Recent analyses have focused on political turmoil, changing attitudes toward death, privacy, national planning, ecology, and the role of corporations in

[4] The Conference Board, *Perspectives for the '70s and '80s,* ed. DuBois S. Morris, Jr. (New York: National Industrial Conference Board, Inc., 1970), p. 3.

[5] See, for example, Herman Kahn and B. Bruce Biggs, *Things to Come: Thinking About the 70's and 80's,* (New York: The Macmillan Company, 1972), and W. A. Hahn and K. F. Gordon, eds., *Assessing the Future and Policy Planning* (New York: Gordon and Breach, 1973).

[6] General Electric Inc., *Developing Trends and Changing Institutions: Our Future Business Environment* (General Electric, April, 1968); also, Earl B. Dunckel, William K. Reed, and Ian H. Wilson, *The Business Environment of the Seventies: A Trend Analysis for Business Planning* (New York: McGraw-Hill Book Company, 1970).

democracy. A final analytical step points out the implications of these trends for the industry and its member firms.[7]

Surveys and Opinion Research

Both the Delphi and literature search techniques place primary reliance on "expert" knowledge and opinion and are therefore most useful in the early identification of trends and the synthesis of seemingly unrelated developments. By contrast, opinion research deals primarily with the levels of awareness, understanding, and concern among the public at large. Hence, opinion research is most useful in measuring the progress of trends already underway and the current salience of specific issues to various groups.

A comparison of the results of "expert opinion" studies with the views of the public at large can be particularly revealing. Studies conducted by The Conference Board in 1968 generated the list of issues shown in Exhibit 8-3, with priority rankings for both "experts" and "public opinion," as shown. (The Vietnam war, by far the most important public concern at that time, is omitted from this tabulation.) There is a fairly high degree of overlap—and perhaps even more than what the terms and data reported suggest—between the issues and priorities indicated by expert judgment and those revealed by general opinion surveys. However, issues such as "the management of change" and "population" that could easily have been reflected in the opinion survey were not found there; further, the experts did not reflect the strong public concern with health care.

It is also important to distinguish between issues of general public concern and those for which significant action by business corporations is desired.[8] A 1972 survey by the Opinion Research Corporation (see Exhibit 8-4) revealed some sharp distinctions between the two. In particular, drug addiction and Vietnam involvement were two issues of strong general concern about which major corporate action was apparently not demanded. By contrast, problems of air and water pollution were thought to be the paramount items for corporate initiative.

An important issue with respect to opinion research for societal scanning is the extent to which a corporation should focus primarily on the views of specific groups—i.e., "special publics"—as opposed to those of the public at large. Sethi and Shocker are perhaps the most forceful proponents of a "special publics" orientation. Their whole approach focuses on "identification of 'reference groups' or individuals whose priorities are to be monitored"

---

[7] Institute of Life Insurance, *Trend Analysis Program,* Trend Report No. 4 (New York: Institute of Life Insurance, 1972). And also see L. L. L. Golden, "Public Relations—'Alerting Management,' " *Saturday Review,* September 11, 1971, p. 70.

[8] Daniel Yankelovich, *Corporate Priorities: A Continuing Study of the New Demands on Business* (New York: Daniel Yankelovich, Inc., 1972); see also Institute of Life Insurance, *The MAP Report: Monitoring Attitudes of the Public, 1971 Survey* (New York: Institute of Life Insurance, 1972).

in order to determine "group preferences."[9] This approach may have some validity for certain purposes; however, it presupposes an objective reality and cohesiveness among social groups that is questioned by many analysts and practitioners.

EXHIBIT 8-3
Salient Social Issues in the United States

Expert Ranking	Issue	Public Opinion Ranking
1	Divisions within U.S. Society	2
2	International Affairs[b]	a
3	Education	7
4	Urban Problems	a
5	Law and Order	1
6	Science, Technology, and Management of Change	a
7	The Economy	4
8	Resources	6
9	Values	a
10	Population	a
11-12	Power/Business-Government Relations	8
a	Personal Affairs	3
a	Public Health	5

[a] Not listed by relevant group.

[b] Strong public concern with the Vietnam War was indicated in the basic study.

Source: Adapted from data reported in "A Special Report from the Conference Board," *Perspectives for the '70s and '80s,* ed. DuBois S. Morris, Jr. (New York: National Industrial Conference Board, Inc., 1970).

Internal Scanning

Although the principal emphasis in scanning is on the collection of information external to the managerial unit, there is an internal dimension as well. As the interpenetrating systems model emphasizes, any social organization is a *part* of its own environment; hence, environmental scanning includes surveillance of internal developments.

A particularly important area for internal scanning is employee attitudes. Some concern with the state of morale and commitment on the part of employees has been a traditional managerial responsibility, but a more modern view emphasizes the importance of discovering broader social developments—as well as reactions to them—through contact with an organization's own employees. Employees entering an organization bring from the larger society a variety of goals, attitudes, and values that inevitably reflect in some ways the changing characteristics of the society itself. Specific groups of

[9] Allan D. Shocker and S. Prakash Sethi, "An Approach to Incorporating Societal Preferences to Developing Corporate Action Strategies," *California Management Review,* XV, No. 4 (1973), pp. 97-105.

EXHIBIT 8-4
National Problems: The Public's Personal Concerns
vs. Their Views of Corporate Priorities

National Problems	Personal Concerns "Here is a list of problems facing the country today. Which two or three of these are *you personally* most concerned about."	Corporate Priorities "Which two or three of these problems do you think large companies should work especially hard on?"		
Air Pollution	46%			63%
Water pollution	31%			46%
Inflation (cost of living)	42%		30%	
Litter and solid waste	20%		25%	
Using up natural resources	15%		21%	
Drug addiction	48%		15%	
Chemical additives or preservatives in food	9%		14%	
Deceptive packaging or labeling	5%		13%	
Employment opportunities for Negroes	6%		12%	
Quality of education	25%		8%	
Slums and urban ghettos	13%		8%	
Racial Difficulties	25%		7%	
Juvenile delinquency	21%		7%	
Involvement in Vietnam	29%		6%	
Discrimination against women	3%		4%	
Draft evasion	9%		2%	
Invasion of privacy	9%		1%	Total Public

"Other answers" and "no opinion" omitted

Source: Public Opinion Index (Princeton, N.J.: Opinion Research Corporation), XXX, No. 8 (1972), p. 3.

employees—by age, sex, or race—may be of special importance with respect to particular issues confronting the organization. At the very least, their attitudes are those of a "relevant public" that management may need to take into consideration.

Of particular interest is employee knowledge of, and dissatisfaction with, specific organizational practices. In the absence of an open and responsive internal scanning mechanism through which such reactions can be brought into the open, appraised, and corrected, pressures build up within the organization and concerned employees turn to outside agencies—the press, or Ralph Nader's "Whistle-Blowers," for example—in order to bring their complaints to light. These tactics may be necessary and appropriate in certain circumstances. Often, however, they simply reflect a failure of the organization itself to adopt internal scanning mechanisms, with the result that valuable internally available information is lost (and unfavorable publicity often generated!). One of the important features of greater participativeness within organizations—which, as further discussed below, is a significant organizational response to an awareness of social involvement—is that it opens up continuing sources of information and contact with individuals who are genuinely knowledgeable about the organization's social involvement.

PROCESS RESPONSES TO SOCIAL INVOLVEMENT

Environmental scanning is in itself a change in the process of management, and the mere collection and dissemination of information undoubtedly produces effects within an organization. As Eli Goldston remarked: "In the process of making this first consolidation of social data from our various operations, we found that our records were less complete and less certain than we had believed. We also found that even inadequate disclosure begins to exert a useful pressure on management to comply with new public expectations as to the conduct of large corporations. It may also be some of the best evidence that management is sincerely concerned and making an effort to meet proper expectations."[10]

It is also possible to identify a variety of more specific ways in which the results of scanning have been utilized to bring about general changes in the internal processes and procedures of the organization, rather than specific new programs or activities. These process responses, which flow directly from the scanning activity itself, are discussed in the following sections.

Cognizance

Managerial awareness of secondary involvement areas and public policy issues as a result of the scanning process leads, at a minimum, to *cognizance*; that is, increased knowledge about the external environment, the existence of "relevant publics" and their viewpoints, social concerns and priorities in-

[10] Goldston, *Annual Report.*

evitably penetrates the internal decision process of organizations, even if no other formal developments occur. It is no longer possible to say "We didn't know. . . ."

General cognizance also increases the likelihood that management will take seriously particular pressures and complaints that may arise. For example, in 1972 McGraw-Hill purchased four television stations from Time, Inc., subject to approval by the Federal Communications Commission. Among those protesting this acquisition were a variety of minority groups who wished to have some influence over both the transfer of ownership and the future operation of the stations. McGraw-Hill's response led to continuing discussions between the company and the various groups, and eventually a substantive agreement guaranteeing both minority jobs and regular programming aimed at minority-group interests. The agreement is monitored by a council of minority-group representatives who meet regularly with local station managers and annually with McGraw-Hill's president.[11]

Reporting

When issues of social involvement and concern are identified through the scanning process, immediate questions arise as to the specific status of the organization with respect to them. How many minority employees are there? What are the sources of pollution? How does the organization interact with local government? and so forth. These questions can be answered through the simple expedient of reporting, often merely by assembling and making available information that is already routinely collected.

As Goldston's previously quoted remarks strongly emphasize, reporting is a significant response in itself, because it acknowledges a "right to know"— hence, a legitimacy of concern and inquiry—on the part of relevant publics and society at large. Reporting thus directly reflects an awareness of social involvement on the part of an organization. Further, of course, open reporting is the first step toward more formal evaluation and appraisal, such as the procedures discussed in the following chapter. However, the importance of reporting alone—of openness, rather than secrecy—cannot be overstressed. The principal focus of the Corporate Accountability Research Group—a Ralph Nader organization—is on the formalization of more extensive reporting procedures concerning corporate social involvement and impact.

Participation

In the McGraw-Hill example above, an initial recognition of "relevant publics" (i.e., cognizance) led to *participation,*—the inclusion of persons and groups concerned with the outcome of managerial activity into the

[11] Theodore Weber, Remarks Presented at Business & Society's Corporate Social Responsibility Conference, October 12, 1972. See also "Kudos for Conscience," *Saturday Review of the Society,* April, 1973, p. 60.

management process itself. Participation is more than simply the receipt of information or the consideration of viewpoints, although these may be early steps in a gradual shift toward participative behavior. An increased emphasis on participativeness, in many forms, is now so pervasive in Western society that we have elsewhere termed this development a *third managerial revolution.*[12] Certainly, participation is a particularly prominent and important response to managerial recognition of social involvement as a result of the scanning process.

We may distinguish briefly between *internal* participation—by persons who might be considered "members" of the managerial unit, such as employees, stockholders, and so on—and *external* participation by "outsiders." Internal participation is more familiar. A primitive form is based upon the benign, but rather naive proposition that subordinates will "feel better" if they have been consulted about some matter involving their activities, even if their consultation has no effect on the eventual results. Proposed methods for incorporating internal participation into the managerial structure of micro-units range all the way from informal and occasional consultation of individual work-groups to extensive changes in the ownership and organization structure of enterprises, such as those suggested by the Scanlon Plan, Kelso's "Two-Factor Theory," and the "co-determination" process now being adopted in Europe.[13]

External participation by persons not specifically involved in a corporation by virtue of employment or ownership is a newer concept. Its most conspicuous—but not necessarily most important—form has been the appointment of "outside" representatives to corporate boards of directors. (Of course, appointment of directors representing established "outside" areas of achievement has a much older history; bankers, college presidents, and leading public figures have often occupied these positions.) The First Pennsylvania Bank of Philadelphia pioneered in this new development by appointing several blacks, women, and young people to its board, and by formally reserving at least one directorship for representatives of each group.[14] General Motors and other large corporations have also moved in this direction. A list

[12] Lee E. Preston and James E. Post, "The Third Managerial Revolution," *Academy of Management Journal,* Vol. 17, No. 3 (September, 1974), pp. 476-86.

[13] See, Louis O. Kelso and Patricia Hetter, *Two-Factor Theory: The Economics of Reality* (New York: Random House, 1967), and Mark Van de Vall and Charles D. King, "Comparing Models of Workers' Participation in Managerial Decision Making," in *Management Research: A Cross-Cultural Perspective,* ed. Desmond Graves, (New York: Elsevier Scientific Publishing Company, 1973), pp. 95-114; Neil Ulman, "The Worker's Voice," *Wall Street Journal,* February 23, 1973, p. 1; David Jenkins, "Industrial Democracy," *New York Times,* May 13, 1973, Financial Section, p. 1; David Jenkins, "Industrial Democracy in Sweden," *New York Times,* October 14, 1973. For a more general discussion, see Max Ways, "More Power to Everybody," *Fortune,* May, 1970.

[14] See John R. Bunting, Jr., "The Need for Broader Representation," in *The Board of Directors: New Challenges, New Directions,* The Conference Board (New York: The Conference Board, Inc., 1972); First Pennsylvania Corporation, *Annual Report* (1972); and "Kudos for Conscience," *Saturday Review of the Society,* April, 1973, p. 60.

of major corporations that had appointed black directors by 1973 contained seventy two company names; some of the directors listed held more than one such appointment.[15] Other organizations have apparently thought this type of move unwise; for example, in 1973 a stockholder proposal for the appointment of outside directors was specifically opposed by the management of IBM.[16] In a modification of this approach, some large firms have created special advisory committees of public representatives that meet with subcommittees of the board of directors and report to the full board on matters of social concern and involvement on their own volition.

A different and more specific form of participation occurs when organizations assign specific decision-making responsibilities to particular representative groups. The Phillips-Van Heusen Corporation, for example, formed a committee on corporate responsibility, composed of managers under thirty five years of age, which is responsible for determining how the shares of stock in various other companies that are owned by the company pension plan should be voted. The committee has unrestricted power to vote proxies, and advisory status regarding the selling of stock. Asked about the participativeness, Phillips-Van Heusen's president commented: "We think that as a company with 15,000 employees they should be participating to a marked extent in making their viewpoint felt. . . ." In the same vein, the company also created a committee on environmental policies, similarly constituted, which reports to the president and which will "police what the company is doing to improve the environment . . . [and] make recommendations to the president on how we can influence our suppliers in any way" to further environmental concerns.[17]

Experimentation

The ability to gather and evaluate information through scanning is limited by existing institutional structures and experience; it is not possible to observe the effects of events that have not occurred. Hence, for example, ability to assess an organization's possible involvement in a particular matter may be limited by lack of awareness and by the reluctance of other organizations to share information. In such cases, as well as those in which no sources of information exist, management may wish to conduct experiments, both with respect to information-gathering devices and to substantive actions.

An example of such an experiment is Atlantic Richfield Corporation's training program for minority employees. Having indentified this area of

---

[15] Milton Moskowitz, "The Black Directors: Tokenism or a Big Leap Forward?" *Business and Society Review,* No. 3 (Autumn 1972), pp. 73-80; and *Business & Society* (MRM Publishing Company), VI, No. 5 (1973), p. 4.

[16] IBM, *Notice of 1973 Annual Meeting and Proxy Statement* (Armonk, N.Y.: International Business Machines Corporation, 1973), pp. 32-33.

[17] Marilyn Bender, "Van Heusen's Hair Shirt," *New York Times,* June 4, 1972. Financial Section.

social concern as being within its sphere of responsibility, the company developed in Philadelphia an experimental program that sought to recruit the hard-core unemployed—ex-convicts, people with no work experience, and those whose parents had no work background—and utilize "some combination of education, attitude training, and work experience that might unlock the door that made social prisoners of these people." Despite actual expenditures of approximately $10,000 per person, very few successful trainees were produced. Yet, Atlantic Richfield's president concluded: "We think we gained experience from this experiment which will enable us to make the next one more fruitful. Perhaps someone else will succeed on the basis of information from our failure."[18]

The Atlantic Richfield example is not an isolated one. Also in Philadelphia, the Smith, Kline & French drug company engaged in a project to rehabilitate the neighborhood surrounding its headquarters. The project involved the conversion of approximately seventy abandoned dwellings into two hundred livable apartments, each with low rent. The concept originated with an SKF executive who became aware of the dimensions of the problem of neighborhood rehabilitation while serving as a member of the City Planning Commission. The SKF effort was successful in rehabilitating the abandoned dwellings, in catalyzing similar programs in the neighborhood area, and in informing the City Planning Commission about new approaches to urban rehabilitation.[19]

Both of these examples must be considered experimental. The Atlantic Richfield program was definitely a trial effort, one that might be extended by that firm or others in other places if appropriate success was achieved. The SKF project was not aimed at rehabilitating all of Philadelphia, much less all areas in which SKF operates, but rather at creating a model of development that might be followed elsewhere. The distinctive characteristic of an experimental approach, as opposed to a more structured substantive response, is that in an experiment one hopes to learn about the situation in the process of dealing with it—and perhaps to learn things that will drastically alter the *way* of dealing with it—and that even negative results can be considered of value in planning subsequent developments. Again, of course, full reporting on experimental projects—failures as well as successes—is essential if the learning experience is to become available to other organizations and groups.

SUMMARY

When large and complex organizations become aware of their involvement with their social environment and the necessity of considering their inter-

---

[18] T. F. Bradshaw, "Corporate Social Reform: An Executive's Viewpoint," *California Management Review*, XV, No. 4 (1973), pp. 85-89.

[19] *Ibid.*

action with external groups and interests as part of the managerial process, their initial response may take the form of *scanning*—systematic information-gathering from the environment. Informal scanning takes place as a consequence of general social relationships, but formal scanning proves necessary as a component of top-level organizational planning and decision making. Formal scanning procedures may be based upon an activity approach in which the primary involvement activities of the organization are traced out to discover their interactions and implications. At the opposite extreme, formal scanning may begin from a societal overview in which major social issues and trends are identified and their implications for a specific organization are then deduced.

The latter approach to scanning is the more comprehensive and imaginative. It involves adoption of a more detached and objective perspective as to the position of the organization within society and creates the basis for continuous reappraisal and possible redefinition of its social role. At the same time, an activity approach is much easier to implement, particularly on an incremental basis, and is much more likely to lead to immediately relevant results. Initial information levels are high; information sources are familiar; known sources of pressure and conflict can be given priority. The very strengths of the activity approach, of course, give rise to its limitations— dependence on *a priori* notions, prejudice with respect to information sources and the merit of particular viewpoints, and over-commitment to established organizational goals. The corresponding shortcomings of the overview approach are its unlimited scope, its tendency to generate abstract and inconclusive results, and the difficulty of relating results to the specific activities and relationships of a particular organization.

In practice, a combination of the two methods—along with internal scanning, revealing the viewpoints and concerns of employees—proves useful. Broad strategic decisions require some elements of the societal overview approach, while incremental and tactical decisions must of necessity be based upon current activities and relationships.

Scanning itself is a response to the recognition of social involvement and leads almost inevitably to greater *cognizance* of relevant publics and societal concerns throughout the organization as a whole. Formal and open *reporting,* often of information already gathered and available within the organization, arises directly in response to the issues raised by the scanning process and reflects the recognition of a "right to know" about various aspects of organizational activity and their social impact. Increased emphasis on the *participation* of individuals and groups at various levels of the management process is a further response to social awareness, and this participation also serves as an additional source of information and, hence, an element in the scanning process itself. Finally, some organizations have found that the only way they can discover the impact of particular actions that they might consider taking is through *experimentation.* Such experiments may be strictly "trial" or "pilot" ventures, or may involve activities pursued as ends in themselves but with a flexible and adaptive approach that acknowledges basic ignorance as to the appropriate extent of involvement and the effects of particular actions.

CHAPTER NINE

Implementation:
Programs and Appraisals

Establishing a formal scanning mechanism, as described in the preceding chapter, is an essential first step in implementing the principle of public responsibility. Through systematic and continuous scanning, an organization identifies its interactions with the larger environment, discovers and evaluates societal trends and concerns, and introduces the results of this analysis into the process of top-level decision making and long-range planning. In addition, the organization may both strengthen the scanning process and implement its results by changing the process of management in various ways—taking cognizance of societal impact, open reporting, increasing participativeness within the organization, and experimentation. All of these responses to the recognition of social involvement bring about changes in the *way* an organization carries out its functions.

Another important type of response to managerial recognition of social involvement is essentially programmatic; that is, once a specific area of interest has been identified, a particular policy is adopted and a program is established to implement it. Although there may be a fine line between some "programs," as we shall discuss them here, and some of the "processes" and "experiments" mentioned in the preceding chapter, there is a clear distinction between the flexible and open-ended nature of process responses and the more specific and structured program responses discussed below.

Both process and substantive responses to social involvement require, of course, systematic appraisal and evaluation. Process responses are generally evaluated directly; that is, the intended process either is underway, or it is not; communication is taking place, reports are appearing, or the reverse; and so forth. By contrast, for substantive programs and major policy changes, a different type of evaluation and control procedure is required. The focus is on the *results* of the action or decision taken and hence on feedback reflecting actual operating implementation, experience, and achievements. Thus, the more ambitious attempts to control and evaluate social involvement activities of organizations have focused on the programmatic and policy responses, some of these attempts are discussed in the second part of this chapter.

PROGRAM RESPONSES TO SOCIAL INVOLVEMENT

Among the major types of program and policy action that may be used to implement the principle of public responsibility, we distinguish four for illustrative purposes: *ad hoc* responses; coalitions; basic structure and policy change; and broadening the planning horizon. Some aspects of organizational specialization discussed in Chapter 4 are referred to again here, although now the emphasis is on examples particularly consistent with the principle of public responsibility as we have presented it.

Ad Hoc Responses

By far the most numerous examples of corporate reaction to social involvement issues can be classified as *ad hoc* responses. Their distinguishing feature is that they focus on narrow and specific external problems and do not become integrated as a regular and pervasive feature of the organization's activity. Most such responses, of course, are justified only in terms of a general sense of "social responsibility." Some, however, could be said to reflect a full acceptance of our own viewpoint, but with respect to individual issues rather than as a central element in the managerial process.

The example of Standard Oil of Indiana's program for the development of minority vendors might be taken to represent a particularly extensive *ad hoc* response. According to Phillip Drotning, vice-president of the company:

American Oil, for at least a decade, had been attempting to implement a minority purchasing program. However, it had been focused in the general office purchasing department, with no sharing of responsibility by the operating departments.

Despite the designation of staff people to seek out minority suppliers, and even the use of an outside black consultant for this purpose, buyers insisted that they could not find qualified minority suppliers, and the program didn't work.

Yarrington [a new executive] turned things around, in his words, "by applying the same principles that made for effective programs in equal employment opportunity." He cites three such principles:

"First—It is not enough for top management to adopt a corporate policy. The line and staff organization must understand that management means what it says.

"Second—The minority purchasing effort must not be perceived as a kind of extra-curricular social venture. It must be integrated into normal corporate operations.

"Third—The search cannot be limited to suppliers who are qualified. The word, instead is 'qualifiable.' Firms must be included that would not meet ordinary standards, but that can—with some assistance—become qualified as suppliers of goods and services."

●   ●   ●

As a consequence of this strategy American Oil in 1971 set a goal of tripling its minority purchases, and far exceeded it. The number of minority suppliers utilized by the company increased from a relative handful to well over one hundred, and the number continues to grow. The company has provided substantial amounts of technical assistance to its minority suppliers, but few direct cost penalties have been involved and most of these are being eliminated as the minority supplier gains experience.[1]

Encouraged by Standard's initial assistance and patronage, many of these firms have now become successful in the marketplace. The same company discovered that minority employment goals were not being met by the Chicago building trades unions engaged in constructing a new headquarters building in Chicago. In response to company pressure, construction crews with approximately one-third minority representation were formed.[2]

An example of a private firm's penetration into the public policy process itself, at a local level, arose in connection with the Quaker Oats Company's decision to locate a new production facility in Danville, Illinois, in 1972. The company was already committed to minority employment goals and was concerned that the minority workers to be hired should be able to live conveniently near to the plant rather than become involved in long commuting distances or local ownership conflicts—both of which would have increased employee turnover and reduced morale. The company therefore made its final

---

[1]Phillip T. Drotning, "Organizing the Company for Social Action," in *The Unstable Ground: Corporate Social Policy in a Dynamic Society,* S. Prakash Sethi (Los Angeles: Melville Publishing Company, 1974), p. 265.

[2]Letter and enclosures from Robert C. Gunness, Chairman and President, Standard Oil Company (Indiana) to Chicago Construction Users Council, dated July 6, 1971.

locational decision conditional upon the city of Danville's adopting a fair housing ordinance that would eliminate any problem of racial discrimination in housing location.[3]

Many other examples of *ad hoc* response could be cited. The distinguishing feature of such responses is that they relate primarily to secondary involvement relationships and do not generate pervasive and continuing changes in the organization's operations within its areas of primary activity.

Coalitions

The formation of coalitions was mentioned in Chapter IV as an important type of organizational response to an increased awareness of social involvement. One of the most ambitious of these was the Urban Coalition, an association of corporate and other interests organized by John Gardner in 1967 in the wake of the civil disruptions and riots of the mid-1960s. This organization has evolved into an independent entity with its own constituency and program, and with a broad orientation toward areas of social concern.

An important example of coalition activity in which the primary functions of private firms were directly joined with public policy goals was the Urban Investment Program established in 1967 by the leading firms in the life insurance industry, a principal source of real-estate financing. The initial announcement, hailed by President Johnson as a "historic contribution to our country," pledged $1 billion in investment funds to ghetto rehabilitation. A second $1 billion, but with a substantially smaller number of participating companies, was pledged in 1969. However, the entire program was terminated in 1971. Many factors—including tight money, the financial collapse of some of the projects funded, and other difficulties—have been cited as reasons for the termination. One critic has charged that "The major reason for the death of the program seems to have been the sharply diminishing returns of the publicity."[4] Whatever the details and explanations involved, this program during its brief life was an excellent illustration of the type of development that might be generated on the basis of our own analysis. The program grew directly out of the primary activities of the firms (making real estate investments), and it reflected an acceptance by them of responsibility for some of the secondary consequences of such activity—specifically, the type, location, and cost of housing available to particular members of society. Improvement in housing conditions and choices has, of course, been an objective of U.S. public policy for several decades. It is of particular in-

[3] "Company Performance Roundup," *Business and Society Review*, No. 2 (Summer 1972), p. 94.

[4] Eugene Epstein, "The Insurance Industry's Quiet Retreat," *Business and Society Review*, No. 2 (Summer 1972), pp. 40-41; see also Stanley G. Karson, "The Insurance Industry Responds," *Business and Society Review*, No. 4 (Winter 1972-1973), p. 72; and Karen Orren, *Corporate Power and Social Change: The Politics of the Life Insurance Industry* (Baltimore: John Hopkins University Press, 1974).

terest that the persons whose range of housing choice was affected by this program were in no way constituents or "special publics" of the corporations involved.[5]

Management's conception of the scope of a relevant problem inevitably affects the dimensions of the coalition to be formed. In Hartford, Connecticut, where the home offices of a number of large insurance companies and manufacturing firms are located, a group of business and political leaders have committed themselves to a holistic approach toward urban redevelopment which will involve all the community segments of a total metropolitan region. The dimensions of the project are suggested in this characterization:

> With Hartford (pop: 158,000), the entire northern half, where the blacks and browns live, will be renewed—not just in terms of housing, but of jobs, of better schools, of improved health care and of social service. The south end, where the white ethnics live, will be improved too. In suburbia, subsidized housing for low- and moderate-income families will be scattered throughout the 28 jurisdictions. And in the outlying region, a new community for 20,000 inhabitants will be built.[6]

The project seems utopian in light of earlier urban rehabilitation failures but is also an experiment to determine whether a broad "everyone wins" strategy will prove more successful than the "band aid" strategies that had heretofore characterized urban renewal programs. Simultaneously, federal, state, and local political organizations as well as business organizations and community groups are gaining expertise and information about their relation to an urban social environment.

A much less ambitious, but interesting example of coalition activity—again in the insurance industry—is the Clearinghouse on Corporate Social Responsibility, established by some of the firms that had been previously involved in the Urban Investment Program. This organization devotes itself exclusively to reporting on the various social performance activities of its members, but its standardization of reporting practices and collection of data provide valuable points of reference for other organizations and industries as well. The 1973 report, covering activities of 147 life and health insurance companies, documents activities in six areas: community projects, contributions, minority and female employment, environmental impact, voluntary personal activities of employees, and investments.[7]

[5] For a comprehensive description of this program, see *Report on the $2 Billion Urban Investment Program of the Life Insurance Business, 1967-72* (New York: Clearinghouse on Corporate Social Responsibility, 1973).

[6] Monroe W. Karmin, "Greater Hartford," *Wall Street Journal,* July 26, 1972, p. 1. See also, Greater Hartford Process, Inc., *The Greater Hartford Process* (Hartford, Conn., 1972).

[7] "Results of the 1973 Reporting Program of Life and Health Insurance Companies on Corporate Social Responsibility Activities" (New York: Clearinghouse on Corporate Social Responsibility, 1973).

Basic Changes in Structure and Policy

Major new commitments and policy directions generally require changes in organizational structure and operating practices. Many process responses—particularly those involving regular participation by nonmanagerial employees and outsiders in the management decision making—are of this character. There are, in addition, many other types of examples of structural adaptation and policy change within organizations.

A particularly interesting case is the relationship between the Joseph Schlitz Brewing Company, of Milwaukee, and a nationwide minority-group organization known as "Operation PUSH" ("People United to Save Humanity"). In 1972 the PUSH organization, headed by Rev. Jesse Jackson, asked Schlitz to commit itself to a 15% minority participation standard *in all of its primary involvement contacts*—not simply with respect to its own employment practices. The 15% figure was developed on the basis of national population data and from estimates of the shares of Schlitz sales accounted for by minority consumers. (The latter point was apparently of primary interest to the PUSH negotiators, who later signed an agreement containing a 10% figure with General Foods.) Following discussions, Schlitz and PUSH entered into a formal, although not legally binding "covenant," whereby Schlitz committed itself to major minority participation in the following areas: employment at all occupational levels; goods and services suppliers; wholesalers; advertising and public relations; finance activities (banking and debt collection); insurance; building and construction; legal work; medical staff; and automobile fleet purchases.[8]   This covenant has obvious and pervasive implications for internal management structure, communication and reporting, and the routine conduct of operations through the Schlitz organization.

A common structural response has been the establishment of "public affairs" or "urban affairs" officers within central corporate staffs. A 1968 Conference Board study found that over 75% of the 1033 companies surveyed had established an identifiable public affairs function. This function was viewed as encompassing five major program areas: government relations, employee political activity, political and economic education, community service, and solution of environmental problems.[9] Another commen-

---

[8] "Covenant between Jos. Schlitz Brewing Co., Milwaukee, Wis., and People United to Save Humanity, Chicago, Ill." (August 17, 1972). Operation PUSH subsequently signed similar covenants with General Foods and Avon Products, Inc., and negotiated others with such firms as the Quaker Oats Company, Carnation Foods, and the Miller Brewing Company. See Douglas W. Cray, "Avon and Operation PUSH in 'Covenant,' " *New York Times,* July 12, 1973, p. 55.

[9] The Conference Board, *The Role of Business in Public Affairs* (New York: National Industrial Conference Board, Inc., 1968), p. 1. See also Owen Kugel, *A Preliminary Evaluation of Major Trends in Corporate Involvement in Urban Problem Solving* (U.S. Chamber of Com-

tator has described this development as establishing "an office of public concern . . . [to] institutionalize the gains and projects of the previous years and encourage those individuals responsible for company operations that have an impact on the public issues to assume the on-going responsibility that is in fact theirs."[10] Although the responsibility and authority of public affairs and urban affairs officers varies widely, their appointments reflect an organizational commitment to continuing and coordinated surveillance of and response to social involvement.

Broadening the Planning Horizon

A final and most significant result arising out of the scanning process is a broadening of the organizational planning horizon so that new criteria of appraisal and new areas of primary involvement activity are introduced.

The integration of scanning into formal long-term planning is probably best illustrated by the General Electric experience. For a number of years, long-term planning at G.E. was based upon a combination of economic and technological forecasts. The resulting plans contained an implicit "other things being the same" assumption with respect to the rest of the social environment. When the civil disturbances of the mid-1960s, along with other developments, demonstrated the invalidity of that assumption, G.E. moved to expand its planning base by incorporating social and political forecasts as well. The result was a four-sided framework—economic, technological, political, and social—within which alternative paths of future development were hypothesized and contingency plans developed. As one of the principals involved has described it: "The sort of strategy that alone seems adequate to the demands of the Seventies starts with a re-definition of corporate purpose, mission and objectives; proceeds to an analysis of the new constraints and opportunities in the changing public expectations of corporate performance; and embraces both the external aspects of strategy (marketing, relationships) and its internal implications (the structure, governance and life-style of the corporation)."[11]

One important result of a broadened planning horizon is that new primary activity opportunities are discovered. Perhaps the outstanding example in

---

merce, September, 1971); Jules Cohn, *The Conscience of the Corporations* (Baltimore: The Johns Hopkins Press, 1971); and George S. Odiorne, *Green Power: The Corporation and the Urban Crisis* (Toronto: Pitman, 1969).

[10] Samuel M. Convissor, "The Role of the Urban Affairs Officer," remarks presented at the Business & Society's Corporate Social Responsibility Conference, October, 1972, p. 5.

[11] Ian Wilson, "Futures Planning: A New Dimension of the Corporate Planner," a paper delivered at the International Conference on Corporate Planning, Montreal (December 8, 1971), p. 9; see also Virgil B. Day, "Business Priorities in a Changing Environment," *Journal of General Management*, I, No. 1 (1973), pp. 45-55. The importance of complete internalization, including necessary structural changes, of social performance programs is strongly emphasized by Robert W. Ackerman, "How Companies Respond to Social Demands," *Harvard Business Review*, July-August, 1973, pp. 88-98.

recent years has been the development of "new towns." The stimulus for the "new town" concept is widespread public and private acceptance of the idea that comprehensive planning with respect to vital community components—housing, industry, education, recreation, and shopping—can create a viable and comfortable living environment. Columbia, Maryland, a new town developed by the Rouse Company, is an example of a private firm's commitment of resources to a new area of primary involvement already identified as a prominent item on the public policy agenda. In a sense, the company's whole activity is a grand experiment, combining new technologies, new concepts, and new patterns of societal development. Public enterprises, such as New York State's Urban Development Corporation (UDC), have also been formed to engage in such new types of activity. In addition, of course, coalitions of public and private organizations have been formed to conceptualize and operationalize such new projects, as in the Hartford example previously discussed.[12]

Other examples of new primary areas of activity derived from major societal and public policy changes are the appearance of numerous small and large firms in the pollution control and waste disposal industry (there activities include actual operations and research and development projects); crime-control and prevention systems; prepaid health protection plans; and contract educational programs, both for elementary-level education and for the hard-core unemployed.

CONTROLS AND APPRAISAL CRITERIA

The omission of systematic organizational controls and appraisal criteria from much of the literature on social involvement—and from many of the examples discussed in the preceding sections—has been a continuing source of criticism, much of it valid. The problem has two dimensions: One is that internal control and accounting mechanisms must be applied to new areas of managerial performance if that performance is actually to be monitored, evaluated, and rewarded. The other is that some means must be found for external reporting and evaluation of the organization as a whole with respect to social performance.

Since the task to be accomplished is relatively new, it is not surprising that the methods for accomplishing it are only beginning to be developed. Some idea of the goal to be attained, however, may be suggested by analogy to the system of accounting procedures used to provide incentives and appraisal criteria with respect to financial resources. The individual departments and units within an organization have, as a rule, budgets, profit objectives, or

---

[12] See special issue, "New Communities: Business on the Urban Frontier," *Saturday Review,* May 15, 1971; and Jack Rosenthal, "A Tale of One City," *The New York Times Magazine,* December 26, 1971, p. 4.

cost-control norms established in terms of their respective tasks. During and after the period of actual operation, reports are submitted showing the results accomplished and the actual expenditures incurred. These reports are then combined to yield an overall account—an income, operating, or profit-and-loss statement—of the financial performance of the organization as a whole. Note two key aspects of this process: The tasks and norms of the various constituent elements are established in terms of the *entire* organization; and the criteria for "success" in any subordinate unit—reducing costs or increasing revenues—are consistent with the criteria for success for the entity as a whole. The difference between revenues and costs for every part of the organization, summed over all parts, yields the profit/loss result for the organization itself. There is thus a direct correspondence between the external criterion of success—as revealed in profit and loss—and the internal criteria to be applied in routine managerial appraisal and evaluation. In principle, the system is self-policing, since the sources of overall success or failure should be identifiable through the internal accounting procedures themselves.

This brief and rather idealized description of the nature of managerial accounting suggests the model of an incentives-accountability system serving both internal managerial and external appraisal purposes. The development of such a system and its integration with the financial accounting systems already in use is the frontier task with respect to the whole area of social involvement at the present time. In this section we review briefly some of the ideas and suggestions that have been put forward in the literature to date and suggest some promising directions for future work.

Internal Reporting and Control

One principle on which all authorities seem to agree is that organizations will actually implement social involvement policies only if two conditions hold: (1) that the policies themselves are forcefully affirmed by top managers on a personal basis; and (2) that managerial performance with respect to these policies is formally reflected in the internal reward structure. Joseph Bower illustrates the first of these points with a story—which may be apocryphal—about a particularly dominant executive who took over the top management position in a large company some years ago: "He observed that he didn't see any black faces in the office building, so he called in the vice-president for personnel and inquired as to why this was so. When he didn't get a very intelligent answer, he said, 'Well, that's all right. Just make sure it's changed by the end of the week.'"[13]

---

[13] Joseph Bower, comments delivered at a Conference on Management and Public Policy, School of Management, State University of New York at Buffalo (May 20-22, 1971), proceedings, p. 134.

Integration of social performance objectives into the reward structure is strongly emphasized by Drotning:

A major roadblock [is that] social goals are perceived as peripheral rather than as an integral element of normal operations. . . . If an employee is held accountable for traditional corporate tasks whose performance will determine his success or failure, and is also urged to undertake social objectives on which his performance is not measured, the result is inevitable. Even the most well-intentioned employee will devote his time and attention to the functions on which his career progress depends. . . . Management communicates as much by what it doesn't do or say as by what it says and does. In fact, behavioral forms of communication are apt to have more credibility than spoken or written forms. . . . Employees are quick to sense what is and is not of serious concern to management, and to reach an inevitable syllogistic conclusion: Management enforces the policies about which it is serious; management doesn't enforce its social policies; therefore, management isn't really serious about its social policies.[14]

Katz has indicated four crucial internal operating variables, any one of which can seriously affect an organization's performance. The variables are: (1) *structure*, including the establishment and formalizing of work flow and communication requirements; (2) *standards*, including the establishment, enforcement, and reinforcement of operating systems, procedures, rules, routines, and policies governing behavior; (3) *evaluation*, including the measurement of performance of individuals, groups, departments, and the total enterprise, and also including the administration of organizational rewards and punishments; and (4) *value reinforcement*, including the legitimization of procedures, plans, and decisions.[15] These variables are the dimensions along which an organization's activities are accomplished, and they provide the necessary element of organizational control over the manner in which the organization acts. The failure of management to have clear channels of communication, well-conceived standards, evaluation based upon those standards, and a process to reinforce those standards with rewards and penalties indicates a loss of management control of the organization. Katz notes: "The enterprise can be thought of as being in control of itself when its structure, standards, and values are clear, when its standards are consistent with strategic objectives and are continually enforced and reinforced; when evaluations are consistent with the standards; and when its members are committed to the values and standards. When these conditions are obtained, members become self-regulating with no need for external policing or threat."[16]

Such optimality is rarely achieved, and continued management effort is re-

---

[14] Phillip T. Drotning, *op cit.;* similar points are stressed by Robert W. Ackerman, *op cit.*

[15] Robert L. Katz, *Cases and Concepts in Corporate Strategy* (Englewood Cliffs, N.J.: Prentice-Hall, Inc., 1970), p. 105.

[16] *Ibid.*

quired to maintain the control necessary for achieving satisfactory performance levels with respect to routine operations and still more with respect to implementing the principle of public responsibility.

Following Katz' analysis, the central element of the control system is the *structure* itself, the channels through which communications flow and reports and directives are transmitted. Perhaps the greatest danger in the assignment of social and public policy responsibility to a "public affairs officer," even at the highest organizational level, is that he and his staff will become removed from the regular operating structure of the organization and hence uninformed about its actual activities and ineffective in changing them. The examples of structural adaptation discussed previously indicate organizational recognition of the key importance of structural arrangements.

Standards can be developed both by internal analysis and scanning and by reference to explicit public policy. However, even when external standards exist—as, for example, in the case of activities monitored by the EPA (environmental pollution), EEOC (minority employment), OSHA (safety and health), and other agencies—managerial initiative is required to apply the external and general standards to its particular operations and to monitor performance. Of course, a particular management may decide to set standards far beyond the limits of external requirements. Such decisions may reflect recognition of an opportunity for innovation and expansion, anticipation of future public policy developments, and other factors.

Structure and standards are joined at the critical stage of internal control—*reporting* and *evaluation.* According to conventional accounting procedures, the preparation and evaluation of routine operating reports is the key element in the allocation of resources within a business organization. These reports answer such questions as: Are costs being maintained at initial budget levels? Are planned output and inventory targets being met? Are anticipated operating profits being achieved? Reporting and evaluation with respect to public responsibility areas is primitive by comparison. The Schlitz-PUSH example previously discussed will obviously require regular preparation of internal reports that will be appraised against the "15% minority participation" standard contained in the basic "covenant" between the parties. HEW and EEOC guidelines are giving rise to similar reporting procedures, as are the local implementation of EPA and OSHA regulations. Nevertheless, it is clear that the type of evaluation being applied to social performance in most instances is rather analogous to the statement "We think we did not lose money this year"—which would hardly meet even the most flexible standards of modern financial reporting.

The final element in the control process, according to Katz, is *value reinforcement;* i.e., implementation through the reward structure. Again, conventional practice with respect to financial variables is well-developed. Managers responsible for major sales and profit increases receive promotions and bonuses; those falling short of targets or over budgets receive minimal rewards or unfavorable transfers. No doubt many large organizations are now beginning to provide suitable rewards for persons specifically responsible for major scanning achievements or for creative insights into new social trends and their implications. And some recent important appointments and promotions appear to reflect past accomplishments in dealing with broad organization-society issues. By and large, however, it does not appear that many organizations have sufficiently internalized the control process for nonmarket areas of accomplishment that effective value reinforcement is actually provided in the internal reward system.

External Reporting: The Social Audit

The other half of the problem of control and appraisal is the external reporting of organizational experience and its assessment against some set of criteria. Again, it is important to recall that corporate rates of return on investment, assets, and sales are widely published and generally accepted as evidence of the quality of performance in primary involvement areas. Market share and other supplementary indicators are also generally available. Nonbusiness organizations also report their operations in terms of expenditure levels and output records with respect to their particular sphere of responsibility—hospital services, crime control, or whatever. The proponents of the "social audit"—a term now applied to almost any effort to present a comprehensive overview of the relationship between any individual organization and its social environment—look toward a parallel development.[17] As Bauer and Fenn state: "In its full vision, the corporate social audit should permit firms to report their performance on issues of current social concern with the same regularity that they report financial performance."[18]

The attempts at more comprehensive corporate reporting represented by the example of Eastern Gas and Fuel, referred to in Chapter 8, are important precursors of the social audit; however, they do not embrace the concept of overall evaluation that is implied by an "audit" approach. By contrast, a number of more comprehensive approaches to the "social audit" itself have been suggested in the literature. Three important areas of development are the preparation of social operations statements, the use of social indicators, and the estimation of overall corporate ratings for social performance.

[17] Major references to this concept include: Raymond A. Bauer and Dan H. Fenn, Jr., *The Corporate Social Audit* (New York: Russell Sage Foundation, 1972); Raymond A. Bauer and Dan H. Fenn, Jr., "What Is a Corporate Social Audit?" *Harvard Business Review,* January-February 1973, p. 37; S. Prakash Sethi, "Corporate Social Audit: An Emerging Trend in Measuring Corporate Social Performance," in Dow Votaw and S. Prakash Sethi, *The Corporate Dilemma* (Englewood Cliffs, N.J.: Prentice-Hall, Inc., 1973); David F. Linowes, "Let's Get on With the Social Audit: A Specific Proposal," *Business and Society Review,* No. 4 (Winter 1972-73), pp. 39-42; Public Affairs Council, *Guidelines for an Internal Corporate Social Audit —A Working Paper* (Washington, D.C.: Public Affairs Council, 1971); Public Affairs Council, *Social Audit Seminar—Selected Proceedings* (Washington, D.C.: Public Affairs Council, 1972); and Meinolf Dierkes and Raymond A. Bauer, eds., *Corporate Social Accounting* (New York: Praeger Publishers, Inc., 1973).

[18] Raymond A. Bauer and Dan H. Fenn, Jr., *The Corporate Social Audit,* p. 1.

Social Operations Statements

Preparation of a "social operations statement" involves an attempt to trace out the impact of the corporation in every possible direction—or, roughly, with respect to every "relevant public"—and then to present the results in a format similar to the conventional income statement for an accounting period. When a full audit on this basis has been attempted, "social benefits" (i.e., revenues) have been estimated for additional jobs, environmental improvement, the value of auxiliary services (e.g., day care centers, health programs), and so forth. These are then balanced against "social costs," such as environmental pollution, staff turnover, and waste materials generated. In the end, a "*net* social impact" of the organization on society is estimated.[19] In a more modest version, only those activities for which dollar values can reasonably be estimated are included. Thus, for example, an illustrative social operating statement prepared by David F. Linowes presented separate accounts for activities "Relating to People," with a "net improvement" balance of $16,000, and those involving "Relations with Environment" with a "net deficit" of $97,000. No attempt was made to combine the two figures.[20]

There are two obvious difficulties with the operations statement approach. One is that of estimating the dollar value of the various types of benefits and costs identified. Although some of the activities and impacts can be evaluated by reference to market equivalents, with appropriate adjustments, others appear to require wild guesses or arbitrary assignments. Evidently, these unsubstantiated figures can have an overwhelming effect on the final balance shown. The second difficulty is fundamentally conceptual. The social operations statement, like the income statement on which it is based, takes the viewpoint of the individual firm; benefits and costs are seen from *its* perspective, and the "benefits" it estimates may appear as "costs" elsewhere in the system. This is a normal state of affairs with respect to routine accounting principles, which aim at measurement of the status of a single organization *vis-à-vis* the rest of the world. However, it is not an appropriate format for evaluating and comparing the *net* social benefits generated by different organizations. Hence, for these two substantial reasons, the operating statement approach does not appear highly promising at the present time.

A less ambitious, but closely related endeavor is the development of "human resources accounting" by Rensis Likert. This analysis assumes that employees are organizational assets and are subject to improvement through such activities as education and health care and to depreciation as a result of

[19] The initial presentation of this approach was Clark Abt, "Managing to Save Money While Doing Good," *Innovation* (January 1972), XXVII; see also the discussion in Bauer and Fenn, *The Corporate Social Audit,* pp. 21-26, and the various *Annual Reports* of Abt Associates, Cambridge, Mass.

[20] A. B. Toan, Jr., "Social Measurement," *New York Times,* March 18, 1973, Financial Section, p. 14.

aging, sickness or injury.[21] Here, again, an attempt is made to develop a comprehensive statement showing the improvement and/or deterioration of the work force for a single micro-unit. This analysis—involving a smaller number of variables and a great deal of market-value comparability at many points—is a more promising, although substantially less comprehensive, application of the audit concept.

Social Indicators

The social-indicators approach attempts to relate the activities of a particular organization to specific indicators of community welfare in such areas as income and employment opportunities, product and service quality, safety and health, crime, transportation, housing, and so forth. The critical assumptions are that social statistics can be developed to reflect the impact of these various areas on the overall "quality of life," and that the activities of individual micro-units can be traced to discover their impact on these indicators. The development and use of social indicators for societal scanning and public policy formation was discussed in both Chapters 6 and 8. The central problem in applying a social-indicators approach is, of course, the availability and reliability of the appropriate indicators themselves. Further, inevitable conflicts among the performance goals measured by the indicators—short-run employment versus long-run social mobility through education, for example—create additional and significant difficulties.

Even in easily measured and generally accepted areas of social concern, complex issues of appraisal arise. Consider, for example, the goal of increased home ownership. A local bank can extend home mortgages to otherwise unqualified applicants in order to increase home ownership in critical local areas; but does the increased ownership resulting really represent an improvement for all persons involved? If so, under what circumstances and to what extent? How could one ever determine when such a program was "too little" or "too much"? In addition, of course, the impact of such a program will be importantly affected by other developments within the same community, and these may reduce or increase the overall social impact of the ownership changes themselves.

On the other hand, the social-indicators approach possesses certain desirable features. For one thing, it relates the performance of individual organizations to a single set of external categories and criteria—those encompassed by the indicators—and hence reflects the basic idea that social involvement involves interpenetration between the organization and society and is not simply a one-directional impact. Further, reference to the *same* set of indicators and issues by numerous organizations should yield reports following comparable formats and hence provide a basis for comparative evaluation,

---

[21] Rensis Likert and William C. Pyle, "Human Resource Accounting: An Organizational Approach," *Financial Analysts Journal,* January-February, 1971.

both among corporations and over time, similar to that provided by financial accounting reports already available.

Use of a social indicators framework for corporate reporting is being facilitated by the publication of more detailed indicator data, both for the U.S. (and other nations) as a whole and for major metropolitan areas.[22] The format for social-indicators analysis displayed in Exhibit 9-1 is drawn from a number of sources and indicates both the range of considerations and some

EXHIBIT 9-1
Social Goals and Indicators

Goals	Indicators
Health & Safety	Life expectancy
	Infant mortality
	Incidence of disabilities and accidents
	Mental health (suicide rate)
	Per capita health expenditures
	Crime rate
Education & Skills	Per capita educational expenditures
	Educational attainment (years)
	Educational performance (test scores)
	Science and arts (expenditures and persons engaged)
Income & Poverty	Earnings (per capita, distribution, and type of activity)
	Incidence of poverty (income and/or living standard)
	Real disposable income (adjusted for taxes and prime changes)
Economic & Social Equality	Distribution of income and earnings (by level, race, sex, and source)
	Social mobility
	Leisure time (availability and use)
Human Habitat	Adequacy of housing
	Neighborhood quality
	Exposure to pollution
	Availability and use of recreation areas
	National defense
Macro-economy	GNP (composition and growth rate)
	Employment and unemployment
	Price stability
Community Involvement & Cohesion	Incidence of social disturbance (riots, demonstrations, etc.)
	Voting participation
	Membership and/or participation in community institutions and activities
	United Fund contributions

Source: This exhibit combines both goals and indicators from a variety of sources. A particularly important reference is *Estimates of Possibilities for Improvements in the Quality of Life in the United States,* by Nestor E. Terleckyj (Washington: National Planning Association, 1973).

[22] Statistical Policy Division, Office of Management and Budget, *Social Indicators 1973* (Washington, D.C.: U.S. Government Printing Office, 1973); and also Michael J. Flax, *A Study in Comparative Urban Indicators: Conditions in 18 Large Metropolitan Areas* (Washington, D.C.: The Urban Institute, April, 1972).

of the key pieces of information that might be involved. As the exhibit clearly indicates, primary involvement activities—such as GNP contribution, employment, and wage payments—can be encompassed within a social-indicators framework, along with qualitative and environmental concerns.[23]

Corporate Ratings

As public concern about the impact of large organizations—particularly corporations—on society has increased, numerous attempts have been made to evaluate, compare, and rank leading institutions in terms of their overall social performance. Church groups, universities, mutual funds, and other investors, in particular, have sought to develop criteria that would enable them to create portfolios of "socially responsible" investments or to utilize their ownership interests in order to promote desirable directions of change.

The ratings developed by such groups generally reflect an attempt to appraise and evaluate organizational responsiveness and performance in relation to a wide variety of public issues and goals. Some of these schemes are simply the results of opinion polls in which respondents, both "expert" and otherwise, are asked to rate lists of organizations on the basis of whatever knowledge or criteria they choose to apply.[24] Other studies—most notably those conducted by the Council on Economic Priorities (CEP)—have involved in-depth factual analysis and careful reporting with respect to particular firms and industries.[25] The latter studies are substantially more informative than the former but suffer from the limitation of their narrower scope—a single industry, and even a single locality, in some instances. However, they overcome the tendency of opinion-poll ratings to be heavily influenced by publicity and public-relations activities.

At least one serious analysis has been made of corporate evaluation activities on the part of "responsible" investors.[26] This study indicates that many important institutional investors have begun to include a "social performance evaluation" in their routine investment analysis; however, no standard approach or rating system appears to have emerged.

---

[23] For further discussion of the use of social indicators for corporate reporting purposes, see Robert L. Clewett and Jerry C. Olsen, eds., *Social Indicators and Marketing* (American Marketing Association, 1974), particularly the contribution of Eugene J. Kelley, pp. 129-45.

[24] See, for example, "Corporate Ratings from Xerox to Con Ed," *Business & Society* (MRM Publishing Company, Inc.), V, No. 12 (1972), p. 1. Regarding annual awards for "Social Action," see "How Social Responsibility Became Institutionalized," *Business Week,* June 30, 1973, pp. 74-82.

[25] Among the Council on Economic Priorities' Studies are: *Paper Profits: Pollution in the Pulp and Paper Industry* (Cambridge, Mass.: The M.I.T. Press, 1972); *Paper Profits: Pollution Audit 1972* (Cambridge, Mass.: The M.I.T. Press, 1972); and *The Price of Power: Electric Utilities and the Environment* (Cambridge, Mass.: The M.I.T. Press, 1973). See also, Council on Economic Priorities, *Economic Priorities Report* (a bi-monthly report).

[26] Bevis Longstreth and H. David Rosenbloom, *Corporate Social Responsibility and the Institutional Investor* (New York: Praeger Publishers, Inc., 1973).

Conclusions

The social audit is sometimes discussed as if it were an internal management report rather than an external document, but this distinction leads to unnecessary confusion. Ideally, a comprehensive audit would serve both purposes and would involve the compilation and synthesis of internal reports in the same way that financial reports are brought together in a consistent summary pattern. However, the necessary framework, standards, and measurements for such an audit are obviously not available at the present time. It thus appears that a considerable difference will continue to exist between internal accounting and control of social impact activities on one hand and external reporting and appraisal on the other. And both internal and external information and evaluation systems will rely to a considerable extent on *ad hoc* selection of areas for analysis, reported data, and appraisal criteria.

The important point is that there is now widespread acceptance of the concept that corporations—particularly large and powerful ones—are involved in complex and interpenetrating relationships with the rest of society. Hence, the notion that these relationships should be explored, measured, reported upon, and evaluated is no longer strange or revolutionary. Therefore, independent and varied attempts to observe and appraise such relationships, both for internal control and for external reporting purposes, should be widely encouraged. As Bauer has remarked, the essential task at the moment is to "get on the learning curve" with respect to this activity, so that future progress can occur. As must be obvious, our own persuasion is that internal and external audits involving almost any approach to formal measurement and reporting—except, perhaps, the compilation of arbitrary and meaningless statements of "net social benefit"—are worthwhile at this time. Such reports may well include, of course, heavy emphasis on the *process* through which decisions were taken and results achieved, as well as an evaluation of the decisions and results themselves.

SUMMARY

The principle of public responsibility can be implemented through a variety of specific programmatic responses involving changes in organizational policy and structure. Some of these implementation responses involve *ad hoc* adaptation to specific issues as a result of conflict or pressure but without introducing major changes throughout the organization. Others involve the formation of coalitions, so that activities previously undertaken individually (or not at all) come to be managed on a collective or cooperative basis. Other and very important responses involve changes within the organization itself, in both structure and policy, so that new areas of responsibility, communication and reporting channels, and control mechanisms are created. Finally, the whole process of scanning and implementation can lead to a broadening of the organizational planning horizon, the adoption of new long-range decision criteria and, perhaps, the opening up of totally new areas of primary involvement.

Any attempt to implement the public responsibility principle, or any other concept recognizing social involvement, requires the development of methods of control and appraisal. These are required for internal management purposes—in order to discover the extent to which objectives are being attained and to reward effective performance—and for purposes of external reporting. At the present time it appears that internal reporting and control systems for social performance in most organizations are still in a primitive state. Only when top management singles out specific areas for measurement and reporting—or when external agencies, particularly those with governmental sanction, are involved—does it appear that formal accountability systems are being developed.

With respect to external reporting and evaluation as well, only a very early stage of development has been reached. However, serious attention is now being given to various concepts and approaches to the preparation of a comprehensive "social audit" for an entire organization, and a variety of experimental projects are underway. It may be anticipated that continued work and interaction between internal and external accounting and appraisal techniques will yield considerable progress and hopefully lead to the development of mutually consistent and comparable formats and concepts in the future.

CHAPTER TEN

Public Responsibility
and Political Participation

The Case Against Political Participation
The Case for Political Participation
Some Guidelines
A Special Problem: The Multinationals
A Concluding Remark

The principle of public responsibility suggests an analogy, as well as an important complementarity, between the market mechanism on one hand and the public policy process on the other. We presume that the members of society directly involved in market contacts with a particular enterprise will reflect their own evaluations of its performance through their market activity. If customers are pleased with the product or service, they will buy larger quantities or be willing to pay higher prices. If they are displeased, they will turn elsewhere for their requirements. Similarly, suppliers, employees, stockholders, and others will evaluate managerial proposals and performance and respond to them with sales, contracts, and commitments—or their opposites. Hence, the market process serves to inform the organization of its success or failure with respect to market-related activities.

The public policy process performs an analogous and complementary role with respect to those performance attributes of the organization not directly mediated through market forces. These may include both certain aspects of primary involvement activities—such as product quality features not readily appraised or understood by the individual buyer—as well as many aspects of secondary involvement. The principle of public responsibility states that the organization should analyze and evaluate pressures and stimuli arising through public policy in precisely the same way that it analyzes and evaluates market experience and opportunity. Both are significant and legitimate.

But now the analogy must be carried one step further. The firm not only gathers market information and responds to market pressures; it also attempts to *shape* and *direct* market forces through product development and procurement, advertising and sales promotion, and the myriad activities that make up its marketing program. And, although there may be specific disagreements and criticisms with respect to the appropriateness of particular activities aimed at influencing the market, it is generally recognized that independent and aggressive marketing behavior is a necessary—and, in most instances, highly desirable—feature of a decentralized and competitive economy.

If it is inevitable and desirable that the firm participate actively in the market process and that it shape that process to its own ends even as it responds to the external market conditions, is it also inevitable and desirable that the managerial unit participate in the public policy process—and, again, for the purpose of accomplishing its own organizational goals? The answer has to be: *Yes*. However, that simple answer only hides the real difficulty of the problem. For, just as lines have been drawn between aggressive competitive marketing on one hand and unacceptable behavior—monopolization, fraud, misrepresentation, and industrial sabotage—on the other, so it is necessary to draw distinctions between responsible and acceptable managerial participation in the public policy process and unacceptable activities involving, for example, deception, subterfuge, and political bribery.

In examining these issues, we first consider the arguments opposing and favoring direct and active management participation in the public policy process, and then suggest some very tentative guidelines that may point toward the distinctions that are required. The discussion is cast entirely in terms of political participation by the business corporation, although it can easily be extended to include organizations within the public sector, local or regional governments, labor unions, and other special-interest groups. Political participation by public agencies and their constituents—e.g., public education systems, health institutions, the Department of Defense—may raise particularly serious questions, since public funds and other resources, such as the service time of public employees, may be used to shape the course of public policy itself.

This brief discussion draws no distinction between the political participation of individual managers and the role of the managerial unit as such. If a person acts on his own out of personal interest and without involving the resources or interests of his organization, then clearly no problem arises. If, on the other hand, he participates with the approval and support of his management associates, then there is no clear distinction between the role of the participating individual and that of the organization as a whole. Further, we draw no distinction here between participation in the electoral process—that is, supporting or opposing candidates because of their receptivity or opposition to organizational interests—and participation in the substance of policy making through public information, persuasion, and direct legislative lobbying.

THE CASE AGAINST POLITICAL PARTICIPATION

The case against political participation by corporations contains two main themes. One is the sheer difference in size and power between the corporate "person" and other natural persons involved in the political process. The other is corporate management's lack of political legitimacy, due to the fact that managers are not duly elected representatives of the public.

Andrew Hacker places these themes within the context of "the familiar pluralist model: a society composed of a multiplicity of groups and a citizen body actively engaged in the associational life. . . . But when General Electric, American Telephone and Telegraph, and Standard Oil of New Jersey enter the pluralist arena we have elephants dancing among the chickens." Further, Hacker notes that although corporate managements may profess to speak for employees, stockholders, or even for themselves, the internal decisions of managerial units are explicitly *not* democratic in the one-man-one-vote sense. Corporations, according to Hacker, "are not voluntary associations with individuals as members but rather associations of assets, and no theory yet propounded has declared that machines are entitled to a voice in the democratic process. . . ."[1]

Although the question of representativeness and legitimacy raises many interesting philosophical issues, the problem of size and power is more important. Even if corporations were fully democratic, and therefore politically legitimate, entities—as, for example, are local and state governments in their *corporate,* as well as their governmental, role—the problem of the relative magnitude and strength of corporate resources *vis-à-vis* those of their opponents within the political arena would remain. Both General Motors and the City of New York are able to spend more money, call upon greater expertise, enlist the support of more individuals and groups, and in general exert greater influence on the public policy process than, say the Acme Manufacturing Company or the Town of Springville. Although the balance may be redressed through the organization of large coalitions of smaller entities, the initial imbalance of size and resources remains critical. Hence, the school of thought represented by Hacker and other critics strongly holds that corporate participation in political life and in the policy-formation process should be strictly limited, and eliminated wherever possible. In this idealistic view, the public policy process should be a democracy of *people,* not of *interests.*[2]

[1] Andrew Hacker, *The Corporation Take-Over* (New York: Harper and Row, Publishers, Inc., 1964), pp. 7-8.

[2] Theordore J. Lowi, *The End of Liberalism* (New York: W.W. Norton and Company, Inc., 1969).

A third criticism of corporate political participation can be found in the traditional managerial literature. Here it is argued that such participation represents an inappropriate function for managers, who should better devote their time to market-oriented goals and the pursuit of profits. Taken at face value, this position seems to be a logical counterpart of the fundamentalist viewpoint; both suggest a narrow conception of both the competence and the legitimate scope of management.

THE CASE FOR POLITICAL PARTICIPATION

The basic case in favor of corporate political participation is that it is an inevitable feature of social life in a large, diverse, and highly organized society. Hence, the political role of the managerial unit should be recognized and guided into acceptable directions. As Epstein states, ". . . corporations, just like other collective social interests, have legitimate political concerns, which are a consequence of organizational goals and which therefore make political involvement inevitable. . . . Corporations should not, as a policy matter, be relegated to the underworld of politics but should be placed on a legal parity with other social interests and be recognized as legitimate political participants in the democratic process."[3]

Certainly the analogy between the public policy process and the market, as two mechanisms by which society directs and evaluates managerial performance, strongly supports the case in favor of corporate political activity. It seems both unreasonable and unwise to expect the managerial unit to monitor carefully the state of public opinion and social preference and to respond quickly and appropriately to changes in tastes and goals, but to refrain from active participation in the process by which those opinions, preferences, tastes, and goals are formed. At a minimum, the corporation can be expected to have access to information that should be taken into account in the process of social choice. If it is indeed true that the establishment of certain standards of air or water quality, for example, will force a particular production facility to close its doors, or a particular product or service to be withdrawn from the market, the fact should be available for consideration during the social decision-making process concerning the standards themselves. In addition, the various "relevant publics" that corporate management may need to take into account in making its own internal decisions may also require representation—and in their role as members of such "publics," although they may also be members of other groups that present other views—in the public policy process. It is naive to assume that the *only* views worthy of consideration are those determined through majority vote by the constituents of elected officials. Hence, Epstein and other supports of corporate political participation insist that it is both inevitable and as legitimate as any

[3] Edwin M. Epstein, *The Corporation in American Politics* (Englewood Cliffs, N.J.: Prentice-Hall, Inc., 1969), p. 16.

other form of representation within a pluralistic social decision-making process. Their concern is that attempts to suppress or deny the existence of this participation may, indeed, force it underground and lead directly to the abuses that supporters and critics alike most wish to avoid.

SOME GUIDELINES

Epstein concludes his analysis of corporate political participation by asking whether or not such activity threatens "to deny on a continuing basis to other interests in the society effective access to and potential influence upon foci of governmental decision making?" His general position is that political activity that threatens such access and influence is not acceptable, whereas activity that represents a particular viewpoint, but leaves avenues of access and influence open to others, is admissible and desirable. He acknowledges the difficulty of drawing specific lines and arriving at firm decisions in individual instances. Since the denial of access to others would tend to create a monopoly of influence for those interests included within the policy process, Epstein's criterion is essentially an anti-monopoly principle with respect to politics. We share this general persuasion and would sharpen it in two respects.[4]

First, it is critical that the participation of managerial interests in the political process be overt and clearly identified, not clandestine or camouflaged. The easiest test of the appropriateness of any activity is one's willingness to submit it to public scrutiny. Certainly, it appears that the willingness of corporate interests—along with other interest groups within society—to appear publicly and openly in support of their views and goals has increased in recent years. Every tendency and pressure in this direction should be encouraged. Correspondingly, criticism of overt political representations as "illegitimate" should be rejected. Suppression of interests and viewpoints can only lead to the creation of genuinely illegitimate—because hidden—processes of communication and influence.

Our second comment has to do with a distinction between the resolution of specific issues or problems within an existing set of "rules of the game" and changes in the "rules" themselves. This is a fine distinction at the margin, although easy enough to recognize at the extremes. For example, the establishment of an environmental protection authority (at any level of government) with power to inspect facilities, issue directives, levy fines, and take court actions amounts to a change in the "rules of the game." Opinions may differ as to whether such an agency is needed within a particular community, how it should be established and administered, and what the scope of its authority should be. By contrast, the setting of specific standards for, say,

---

[4] For a similar viewpoint see The Conference Board, *The Role of Business in Public Affairs* (New York: National Industrial Conference Board, Inc., 1968).

stack emissions or liquid effluent discharges is a specific task confronting such an agency; and, again, there may be differences of view about both the level of standards to be established and the means of monitoring or correcting them.

An individual managerial organization may have a specific, overt, and perfectly valid position on both issues—the existence of the agency itself and the specific standards, if any, to be applied—and both positions may be appropriately represented in public policy debates. The problem arises, however, when there is a deliberate attempt to change the "rules of the game" themselves under the guise of merely resolving a specific problem within the existing system. For example, an organization—and, particularly in the environmental protection field, it is as likely to be a governmental unit as a private firm—may attempt to resolve a specific standards question in such a fashion that the responsible agency is precluded from setting *any* standard, from conducting inspections, or from placing sanctions upon violators. If so, it is not the specific regulation but the "rules of the game" themselves that are under attack.

Again, it is perfectly legitimate to attack "the system" in all of its aspects, and the "rules" are—and should be—changed in response to changing circumstances. However, it is *not* legitimate to attack the system as a whole through the subterfuge of merely altering some specific operating feature. Again, the distinction may be difficult to draw in practice, but one way to put it would be that not only the *source* of participation in the political process— i.e., the firm, industry, or organization responsible—but also the true nature and *purpose* of participation, should be publicly acknowledged.

Our conclusions with respect to managerial participation in the public policy process, therefore, come down to a few very simple points. Such participation is inevitable and legitimate; and, as public policy becomes an increasingly important consideration in the process of management, such participation can be expected to become more widespread and significant. Our caveat is that such participation should be acknowledged for what it is—both with respect to source and with respect to purpose—and that it not be conducted in such a fashion as to exclude other views and interests from equal participation in the process itself.

A SPECIAL PROBLEM: THE MULTINATIONALS

In an earlier chapter we raised the question: "Who is the public that has the public interest?" At that time we wished to draw attention to the number of different and not necessarily harmonious elements within society, and the need to draw a distinction between the objectives of particular groups on one hand and goals arrived at by general consensus or compromise within society at large on the other. Here we raise the question again, but with a different emphasis. Suppose that a particular managerial unit operates in more than one society. How is it to relate and balance the goals and standards of several different social environments in arriving at internal decisions and policies, in appraising its own performance, and in its political participation?

These questions can arise, of course, in organizations operating in different parts of a single country, and even in different socio-economic contexts within smaller geographic areas. At various times in the recent past there has been considerable conflict among states and regions of the U.S. because of attempts by some areas to lure manufacturing and service facilities from other areas by means of tax subsidies, public loans, and other special incentives. Even today there are conflicts within and between firms operating in different regions with respect to employment practices—particularly minority employment and fringe benefits—that reflect, in part, differences in the social environment and public policy in different parts of the country. Nevertheless, the problem of operating in multiple societies, each of which may have its own internally valid public policy, is most clearly evidenced in the case of multinational enterprises.

The traditional model of international business operations has, of course, been based upon the concept of exploitation; that is, it has been assumed that foreign plants and branches were operated in the interest of the parent organization and hence for the benefit of the "home" country, whichever it may be. The historical and ideological connection (both favorable and unfavorable) between political imperialism and foreign economic activity both supports and reflects this viewpoint.

In the well-known book *Sovereignty at Bay*,[5] Raymond Vernon contrasts the exploitation model—summarized as "the world is our oyster"—with a policy of socio-cultural adaptation referred to as "when in Rome . . ." Although he finds some validity in each of these conceptions, both are of limited usefulness for analyzing the actual practice of multinational organizations. Yet the alternative to these two approaches is difficult to identify. Rejection of the exploitation model, he notes, "does not mean that a rational parent (company) would be expected to make its decisions on a basis consistent with the achievement of the largest social gain for each host country. This, of course, would be impossible, if only because the social gain to one country may be the social loss to another. It does not even mean that the decisions of the parent will approximate those that would be taken according to globally conceived criteria of social gain. . . ."[6] Vernon believes that "governments—especially the U.S. government—will be obliged to convert issues they had once thought domestic into issues of international concern. . . . Initially, this outcome may seem a trifle strange. Its strangeness

---

[5] Raymond Vernon, *Sovereignty at Bay* (New York: Basic Books, Inc., 1971). Another important reference and guide to the rapidly growing literature in this area is David H. Blake, ed., "The Multinational Corporation," *The Annals*, CDIII, September, 1972).

[6] Raymond Vernon, *Sovereignty at Bay*, p. 135.

declines rapidly, however, if one accepts the view that the accountability of multinational enterprises is international for certain purposes. . . . The response is bound to have some of the elements of the world corporation concept: accountability to some body, charged with weighing the activities of the multinational enterprise against a set of social yardsticks that are multinational in scope."[7]

Rephrasing Vernon's observations for our own context, they imply that even if the public responsibility principle were fully incorporated into the domestic decision process of private management, the increasing international involvement and impact of U.S. organizations—and the U.S. activity of foreign companies—would raise a host of new and difficult issues. When both the maintenance of domestic employment and income *and* the spread of economic development and technical progress to other countries are recognized public policy goals—the former the stronger goal in the home country and the latter the more salient abroad—does public responsibility favor the expansion of the domestic or the foreign manufacturing plant?

In this thorny and controversial area we are bold enough to offer a few observations. One is that careful delineation of the *scope* of managerial involvement in various societies may, by itself, create an atmosphere within which some of these apparent dilemmas can be more clearly appraised and resolved. A prominent issue in recent years has been the extent to which companies headquartered in one country (the U.S., in particular) should use their international operations to influence domestic policies in others. Specific examples are the alleged role of I.T.T. in the overthrow of the Allende government in Chile in 1973, and the frequent demand that U.S. firms take the lead in bringing about a major social transformation—the elimination of racial discrimination—in South Africa. The first of these, along with many similar allegations involving various countries and companies over the years, has been widely condemned as an unwarranted use of corporate authority and resources; the second has been criticized for precisely the opposite reason.

It seems to us that racial policies in South Africa and the form of government adopted in Chile are matters clearly outside the scope of U.S. parent companies, although entirely within the scope of their subsidiaries domiciled in those countries. But for each of the latter, public policies of the local society should be controlling. Further, for the parent company, the relevant (U.S.) public policy is clearly that companies headquartered here should not use their resources for subverting legitimate governments or promoting social upheaval elsewhere. Indeed, such activities are clearly "out of scope" so far as the "rules of the game" in this country are concerned. The fact that our own society is specifically *not* committed to a policy of forcing its own views and practices upon others is particularly significant.

[7] *Ibid.*, p. 284.

Two subsidiary points are also worth noting. Should it become official U.S. policy to interfere in the affairs of other countries—as, for example, in wartime or in the limitation of strategic shipments during the Cold War period—then, of course, parallel behavior by the management of U.S. companies is appropriate. Second, and perhaps more important, conspicuous and highly questionable corporate influence in any country (including the U.S.) and on any issue cannot fail to create a general impression that corporate influence, legitimate or not, can and should be used in other countries and for other purposes. If it were acceptable for U.S.-based multinationals to participate in revolutionary movements in Chile, it would also be acceptable for them to take the initiative in bringing about social change in South Africa. Large corporations, domestic or multinational, that are willing to take the law into their own hands will probably get more, and very different, laws to enforce than they originally anticipated. As for discovering what is, and is not, within the scope of corporate involvement and consistent with public policy in various societies, the scanning function remains of critical importance. Further, the multinational firm will be concerned not only with scanning in a greater variety of societies, but also with respect to different types of issues—e.g., international corporate chartering under United Nations auspices—as compared to its domestic counterpart.

A different type of issue is raised when there are genuine and substantial benefits to be generated in one society, and their opposites (or nothing) in another, as a result of multinational corporate activity. Casual observation suggests that in many such situations there is substantial room for bargaining and compromise among all parties and that some of the alleged "dilemmas" of the multinationals arise from failure to anticipate conflicts and develop satisfactory bases for negotiation and compromise. Further, when there is a direct conflict between corporate actions and public policies in two countries, the political authorities in *both* may need to become directly involved, along with the corporation, in the process of resolution. Actions of U.S. parent companies, following American law, that prevented sales by their European subsidiaries to certain third parties—China, U.S.S.R., Cuba—in spite of the economic and political objectives of the European governments involved, illustrate the problem perfectly.[8] Issues such as these become, in the end, matters for political negotiation between the governments concerned. Direct policy conflicts among several host societies—or action decisions that cannot possibly conform to the goals of all of them— must be referred back to the international political mechanism for resolution. The corporate entity alone is not capable—and also not authorized—to resolve such problems.

[8] Neil W. Chamberlain, *The Limits of Corporate Responsibility* (New York: Basic Books, Inc., 1973), Chap. 8.

A CONCLUDING REMARK

The modern large corporation is clearly a prominent institution—some would say *the dominant* institution—in our society. Although it has been described by a leading social commentator as "more and more like a species of dinosaur on its lumbering way to extinction,"[9] the symptoms of corporate morbidity are not conspicuous and demands for euthanasia, still less public execution, are hardly deafening. In fact, as Jacoby has pointed out, public insistence that corporations take on greater responsibilities within society implies the continued legitimacy and strength of the corporate entity itself.[10] There is very little enthusiasm for formal nationalization in this country, and even in other parts of the world the notion that public ownership has more than a cosmetic effect on managerial organizations is widely questioned. (Ownership changes can, of course, have substantial effects on the distribution of income and of political and social power.) Nor is a significant expansion of public regulatory authority over private business activity generally thought to hold the key to improved economic and social performance.[11]

Yet the current state of affairs is not entirely satisfactory. There *are* demands for increasing corporate involvement in society, and these demands come not only from dissident minorities and pressure groups but also from serious and concerned executives, employees, stockholders, and public officials. The fact of corporate influence and power in society is simply too conspicuous to be overlooked. The deleterious effects of corporate activity have been voluminously documented; examples of improved performance are numerous, and the possibilities for further improvement ubiquitous and highly visible. In short, the *fact* of corporate interpenetration with society is very generally recognized, although the term itself has not been previously used in this context.

Given the fact of interpenetration, what is to be done? The executive who responds, "It's none of my business," will probably have to look for another job. Public relations and legalistic responses were discredited long ago; and attempts to bargain with particular interest and pressure groups in order to dispose of their demands seem to encourage the growth of both groups and demands over time. After surveying these traditional responses to social

[9] Irving Kristol, "The Corporation and the Dinosaur," *The Wall Street Journal,* February 14, 1974.

[10] Neil H. Jacoby, *Corporate Power and Social Responsibility* (New York: The Macmillan Company, 1973).

[11] Ralph Nader and his associates may be the strongest current supporters of increased regulation, and this in spite of their penetrating criticisms of previous regulatory experience. For some of their proposals and viewpoints, see Ralph Nader and Mark J. Green, eds., *Corporate Power in America* (New York: Grossman Publishers, 1973).

issues, Votaw and Sethi ask, "Do we need a new corporate response to a changing social environment?" And their answer is clearly affirmative.[12]

But the new response itself has not been forthcoming. Instead, diverse behavioral and structural developments have taken place without any clear pattern or coherent philosophy. Some of these, such as philanthropy, have involved traditional corporate activities; other, such as the appointment of minority directors, have involved new ideas. All have been motivated by a vague sense of "social responsibility," although even its strongest supporters have been hard put to explain what that term means or how it can be used to identify specific areas of appropriate—or inappropriate—corporate behavior.

The principle of public responsibility developed in this book is offered as the "new response" called for by Votaw and Sethi. We believe it builds upon the socialization process that has already taken place in our society, particularly within larger firms and among younger corporate executives, and offers both a rationale and a guideline for managerial behavior. It overcomes the two major defects of the "social responsibility" doctrine by defining the scope of managerial concern in terms of the areas of primary and secondary involvement and by recognizing the public policy process as the source of goals and priorities for managerial activity not mediated by the market.

Implementation of the public responsibility principle places heavy emphasis on information-gathering and formal reporting, both for internal corporate decision making and for external dissemination. The use of inter-firm and firm-society comparisons is particularly stressed, leading to an increased awareness of the need for societal guidelines and performance standards. Furthermore, corporations should be encouraged to participate in the development of such standards and of the public policies underlying and embodying them.

We have no illusions that these ideas—or any others, for that matter—will quickly solve all the problems of the world; or even that careful consideration of our analysis will make specific managerial decision processes very much easier or subject to greater social acclaim. However, there seems to be a widespread feeling in our society that, without any major social upheaval, a great deal of managerial activity could and *should* be carried out in a manner that contributes somewhat more to the public interest. And this feeling seems to be as common among managers themselves as among their critics. If our analysis should provide any stimulus at all toward improving managerial social performance in this sense, it will have served its purpose.

[12] Dow Votaw and S. Prakash Sethi, "Do We Need a New Corporate Response to a Changing Social Environment?" *California Management Review*, XII, No. 1 (1969), pp. 3-31; reprinted in Dow Votaw and S. Prakash Sethi, *The Corporate Dilemma* (Englewood Cliffs, N.J.: Prentice-Hall, Inc., 1973).

Index